THE WIND, THE FOUNTAIN
AND THE FIRE

THE WIND, THE FOUNTAIN AND THE FIRE

Scripture and the Renewal of the Christian Imagination
The 2020 Lent Book

Mark Barrett OSB

BLOOMSBURY CONTINUUM
LONDON · OXFORD · NEW YORK · NEW DELHI · SYDNEY

BLOOMSBURY CONTINUUM
Bloomsbury Publishing Plc
50 Bedford Square, London, WC1B 3DP, UK

BLOOMSBURY, BLOOMSBURY CONTINUUM and the Diana logo are
trademarks of Bloomsbury Publishing Plc

First published in Great Britain 2019

A catalogue record for this book is available from the British Library

Library of Congress Cataloguing-in-Publication data has been applied for

ISBN: PB: 978-1-4729-6837-1; ePDF: 978-1-4729-6839-5
ePUB: 978-1-4729-6836-4;

2 4 6 8 10 9 7 5 3 1

Typeset by Deanta Global Publishing Services, Chennai, India
Printed and bound in Great Britain by CPI Group (UK) Ltd, Croydon CR0 4YY

To find out more about our authors and books visit www.bloomsbury.com
and sign up for our newsletters

For my parents,
Douglas Keith and Jean Margaret Barrett

CONTENTS

INTRODUCTION

'How do you cope with Psalm 78?' the young nun asked me.

I promise you, not every conversation between Benedictine nuns and monks has to do with sacred texts and spiritual aspirations. We can time-waste in gossip along with the best. But this question, asked some 40 years ago, came from one monastic newcomer (or 'novice') to another, and novices tend at least to aim for more edifying discussions.

Psalm 78 is the longest account of Israel's sacred history in the Old Testament Hebrew hymn book, the psalter, as the book of Psalms is often called from its Latin title *psalterium*. 'Give ear, O my people, to my teaching; incline your ears to the words of my mouth', the psalm begins (Ps. 78.1). One point being made by that young nun is that, with it being 72 verses in total, inclining one's ear to the entirety of Psalm 78, to say nothing of lending one's mouth to its words to recite them in choir, is a significant test of any novice's monastic endurance. Israel's desert wanderings took God's people 40 years, we are told. This psalm, when you first meet it full-length in worship, can seem to be taking at least as long. 'Are we there yet?' the heart murmurs.

Monastic men and women spend more hours of the day sitting with the psalms than we do in most other activities.

I suppose you might call us professional psalm-singers. So it is very far from unreasonable for one monastic to ask another about how he or she approaches prayer with the psalms. It's the kind of necessary specialist conversation that, between those with a passion for any endeavour, indicates a healthy approach to improving an individual's skills in their chosen field; a good thing in most people's books.

And so, when I was asked about the challenges of approaching this lengthy psalm, I might – for example – have pointed my novice friend to Psalm 78's opening words 'Give ear ... to my teaching', echoed very directly in the first words of the Rule of St Benedict: 'Listen, my child, to my teaching, and incline the ear of your heart.' One way to appreciate the psalms is to recognize the various ways in which their perspectives, language and images inform so much of our Christian tradition, including the 'Rule', or 'way of life', written for monastics in the sixth century by St Benedict of Nursia; the classic Christian text that continues to inspire the life of Benedictine monasteries to this day.

Alternatively, my answer that day might have targeted the colourful imagery of divine action bringing help to God's chosen ones that runs through the psalmist's account of Israel's desert journey. In Psalm 78, God and God's chosen people Israel are portrayed in a species of salvific dialogue, with the whole natural order becoming the vehicle of that conversation. And so, in this psalm, when the wind blows it does so because it was summoned by

God to bestow the blessing of food in the wilderness on a
hungry nation:

> ... he sent them food in abundance.
> He caused the east wind to blow in the heavens,
> and by his power he led out the south wind.
>
> (Ps. 78.25-26)

The dry, desert landscape through which God's people
venture is suddenly watered by fountains springing from
the rocks, shattered by earthquake at the Lord God's
command:

> He split rocks open in the wilderness,
> and gave them drink abundantly as from the deep.
> He made streams come out of the rock,
> and caused waters to flow down like rivers.
>
> (Ps. 78.15-16)

And, through the trackless wilderness, the compassion of
God blazes like a column of raging fire ahead of his chosen,
guiding them towards their ultimate destination:

> In the daytime he led them with a cloud,
> and all night long with a fiery light.
>
> (Ps. 78.14)

The attitude of attentive listening, of receptivity before
God's word, inculcated by our centuries-old Benedictine

way of life; the capacity of the language and imagery of
the psalter, the Book of Psalms, to perform evocatively
by stirring up a great wind from God, breaking open a
fountain of living water within our hearts, inflaming us with
a fire that cannot be easily quenched – these might have
offered me the beginning of an answer when I was asked
about Psalm 78. But to my embarrassment, I had to admit
to the novice nun that my own monastery did not attempt
to 'cope with' Psalm 78, whole and entire. At that time,
it was delivered to us in bite-size portions, spread over
several days, and then only during Lent. As a consequence,
I really had never thought about the wider implications
of the question she was asking. I won't tell you what my
interlocutor said in response to that. Suffice it to say that
any emerging aspiration on my part to guru status was
rapidly – and quite rightly – dismissed.

More recently, my brethren and I have mended our ways.
We now trek through the full extent of this psalmic tale of
Israel's infidelity to our faithful God throughout the year, on
every other Thursday morning – though we do take a brief
pause about halfway through Psalm 78 in an attempt, not
always wholly successful, to get the reciting note back up
again. Now that I do have a regular experience of attempting
to cope with this demanding psalm, I can (somewhat
belatedly) attempt the answer I should have been ready to
offer forty years ago to my fellow monastic novice. This
book is a version of that answer; though I must allow that
the answer has now grown a fraction longer than it might
have been all those years ago! And I suppose it has done so
not least because I write now with an awareness that it isn't

only the professional psalm-singers of our monasteries and religious houses who may struggle from time to time to find their way into some of our sacred texts. I hope that readers who perhaps have less time to spend among the psalms and the rest of scripture than we nuns and monks have in our monasteries may find something of value in the pages that follow.

In *The Wind, the Fountain and the Fire* I invite you to join me in noticing in the psalms and more widely across the pages of the Bible – particularly the magnificent sequence of Lenten Sunday Gospel texts – some of the things it would have helped me to be aware of when I was asked about praying with Psalm 78, 40 years ago. The question I ought to have been asking is: how does any of us find her or his way into scriptural texts? Where do we discover the wind of the Spirit, the fountain of living water and the fire from which God speaks, among the printed pages of our Bibles? Looking back, I realize that it is the regular practise of psalmody – singing the psalms in community – along with a daily attending to the sacred reading of scripture during worship and in personal prayer, that rubs away at the edges of my ignorance, slowly eroding some of my hardness of heart. Repetition opens doors. One of the ways that it does this, I now appreciate more fully, is by bringing my experience of praying the psalms right up against my reading of the rest of the books of the Bible, especially the New Testament and the Gospels. The images and word-pictures I encounter throughout the day in the psalms I sing among my brethren in the monastery choir resonate with the central themes of Jesus' message of salvation in the Gospels; at the same time, the Gospel sayings and actions of Jesus are reflected back onto the texture of our psalmody, enriching and renewing its ancient insights.

Finally, and most importantly, praying the psalms in the context of regularly reading the scriptures involves those who do this in being changed by what we do: scriptural prayer is, we might say, a performative prayer, a thing we do. In singing the psalms, or reading the Bible prayerfully, we ourselves are most certainly doing something; but perhaps the more important dimension of this activity is one that is harder to notice and perhaps almost impossible to quantify – because as we 'do' the psalms, as we perform them, something is being done by the psalms to us. As I work on the Bible, the word of God works upon me. As I read the word, the furniture in the house of my heart is being moved around, or even replaced completely; my imagination is being reshaped in the image of Christ.

THE CLIMATE OF MONASTIC PRAYER

In numerous ways, praying with the psalms constitutes the 'climate of monastic prayer', to borrow a felicitous phrase from Thomas Merton, the American Cistercian writer. I find the metaphor of climate appropriate and illuminating in this context. A climate is neither a single event, such as a rainbow or a thunderstorm, nor a solitary season of good weather or bad. Rather, we use the term to characterize a slowly shifting backcloth against which individual events – the rain and the shine – play out; almost an environment within which they achieve their specific character. 'Climate' is the name more of a whole container than it is of any one of the contents. In this sense, you might say that the psalms provide the environment within which monastic prayer, perhaps even the whole of monastic life, takes place. They are simultaneously among its most salient features, occurring prominently in public monastic prayer from very early in the morning through to the end of the day, every day of the year.

A monastic community at prayer, and individual monks and nuns in their personal scriptural reading and reflecting, move constantly between tasting the language of the psalter and encountering the poetry and narrative of the Old and New Testaments more broadly. In living this way, monks and nuns strive to enact in our approach to living among the psalms and the scriptures a version of the earliest Christian understanding of the book of Psalms, as both a gateway into and a summation of all the other books of the Bible: in the psalms we encounter the 'climate of biblical prayer'.

This dynamic understanding of the relationship between scripture and psalmody is well expressed by Athanasius, a fourth-century bishop of the Church in Alexandria and a commentator on the psalms. In a letter he wrote to his friend, the deacon Marcellinus, about praying the psalms, Athanasius explains that he understands each book of the Bible to be like a garden that grows just one special kind of fruit – the fruit of moral insight, of spiritual depth, of encouragement to charity, and so forth. He contrasts the book of Psalms with the rest of the Bible in this regard, because for him the psalter is a different kind of garden. Besides its own special fruit, the poetry of praise, the garden of the psalms also grows some of the fruit of all the other gardens. To put the same point in another way, in prayer the psalms take us to all the places that God's activity touches the whole of his people's lived reality. Psalmic poetry explores and celebrates (as well as bemoaning and lamenting) the shape of Israel's numinous, tumultuous encounter with God, the Lord of history. Other Christian thinkers over the course of many centuries have offered parallel appreciations of the power of the psalter. For the great thirteenth-century Catholic theologian Thomas Aquinas, the psalms can be said to embrace the whole of theology. For the fifteenth-century German reformer, Martin Luther, they are to be understood as a 'little Bible', the whole revelation in miniature.

At the same time that these 150 psalms open gateways into the entire range of the scriptural revelation, they can also be said to articulate interior happenings in our human hearts. The psalms put into words the messy complexity of how you and I experience our relationship with God, with ourselves and with one another; stepping into the swampy, wild places of our private emotions and our feelings about ourselves. For the fifteenth-century Genevan reformer John Calvin, they map the landscape of all the parts of the soul. In his commentary on the Psalms, he writes of them as being like a 'mirror to the soul', employing a metaphor that is widely supported by Christian writers before and since his time. There is not an emotion of which any one can be conscious that is not represented somewhere in the psalms, Calvin tells us. Athanasius, who may perhaps not have shared Calvin's views in every respect, agrees with him here: 'within the psalter are represented and portrayed in all their great variety the movements of the human soul', he writes. Athanasius sees the psalms as a set of pictures in which we see ourselves portrayed, 'and seeing, may understand'.

So, the psalms guide us towards the key themes of revelation, and they help uncover the truths of our own hearts. These are important perspectives on why we might wish to pray with the psalms. They can enable the one who approaches this task to have an initial sense of why such ancient poems continue to command contemporary involvement. But the challenge posed by the novice nun's question is a real one. *How do you cope with Psalm 78?* In other words, how does someone who is new to these venerable but challenging prayer-poems start to find her or his way into using them as their personal prayer? The issue doesn't apply only to that one specific psalm. Many of the ideas we encounter as we enter the world of the psalms, old though they are, are very new to us and can appear strange or indeed off-putting. The psalter is a large collection of very ancient texts, written by many anonymous authors at different times and in a variety of human circumstances, even the most recent of which is far older than the two millennia of the Christian era. It's hard to think of another example of such a varied text of such antiquity that still informs the thought and language of contemporary people. To engage effectively with such material, especially at a personal level, it can be helpful to be offered some ways into a deepened understanding of what they are about and why they matter.

Prelude to Lent:
Stepping into the Story of Scripture

Because monasteries are places explicitly intended to prepare people to engage in the challenge of praying with the psalms and the scriptures, our Rule of life prescribes a period of initial training in some fundamentals of our way of living and praying. This lasts several years, and offers monks and nuns the support of mature monastic practitioners as well as academic specialists, such as scripture scholars, as we seek to understand how prayers and activities often far removed from our twenty-first-century everyday can be gateways to the sacred for us today. Although the way we approach this process of formation in monastic living and praying with the scriptures is different today from the approach taken in the sixth century when St Benedict wrote his Rule for Monks, there is a direct line of continuity in the recognition that when we pray with an ancient text, what we do and why we do it is not always immediately obvious.

The book of Acts in the New Testament, tells of an encounter between one of Jesus' first followers, the apostle Philip, and an Ethiopian court official that touches on this very point. In chapter 8, Philip is on a whirlwind preaching tour of Palestine in the very earliest days of the Christian movement when he encounters the high-ranking foreigner deeply engrossed in reading the scriptures, what we would now call the Old Testament. It is the book of Isaiah that has seized the official's attention. 'Do you understand what you are reading?' Philip asks him. The question is as old as the Bible, and as new as today. Thankfully, so is the answer the official gives. He replies, in words we all might claim as our own: 'How can I, unless someone guides me?' (Acts 8.31). The story tells us that the guidance in scriptural prayer Philip offers the court official leads him to change his life, and be baptized as a follower of Jesus. Clearly, to be guided into reading and praying with scripture involves entering a very personal kind of relationship with the text that is set before us. It requires being prepared to be affected by what we read, and being prepared to change in response. But, before any of this is possible, we need some guidance in how to read in this way. It is not the way that we have become accustomed to reading today, as we skim and scan our news websites or text messages on the train to work.

UNLESS SOMEONE GUIDES ME

There is an Old Testament story that can be read as a kind of narrative version of the Ethiopian official's question; an illustration in practice of what kind of guidance we all need if we are to engage in an appropriate way with the sacred texts of psalms and scriptures, and be able to respond to them. The story is told at the beginning of the first book of Samuel, in the third chapter, and it tells of the first direct encounter of the young boy Samuel with God; this is the same Samuel for whom the book is named and who will go on later as an adult to become an Old Testament prophet of great stature.

The story is set in the days before Israel became a nation, when God's people were living as a loose association of tribes. Prophetic leaders play a significant role in the life of the tribes of Israel, who worshipped God at this time at a shrine in the town of Shiloh. But the most important context for our reading of this story is the fact that the boy Samuel is presented to us by the scriptural text in the first few chapters of this book as the ultimate insider as far as the religion of ancient Israel, the religion of the Old Testament, is concerned. If anyone was to know how to engage with messages from God, the young Samuel is the person.

Samuel's mother, Hannah, has prayed to God for his conception and birth, promising that her child will be given over to God from his very first breath. As a baby, Samuel is dedicated to God by his parents in God's shrine at Shiloh as soon as he is weaned; 'as long as he lives, he is given to the LORD', says Hannah (1 Sam. 1.28). This is a boy, we are being told, whose fundamental direction of life is oriented towards Israel's God. Touching details of the child Samuel's young life as a temple minister are offered in the stories that follow; what is absolutely not in doubt is that 'the boy Samuel continued to grow ... in favour with the LORD and with the people' (1 Sam. 2.28). Mentored by Eli the senior priest of the shrine of God in Shiloh, ministering daily before the Lord on behalf of God's people, the boy Samuel is presented as God's young man in a way that few of us could ever claim to have been at any stage of our lives.

So when in chapter 3 of the story the Lord calls personally to the young Samuel, it is a shocking thing that happens next. The storyteller introduces an initially tranquil scene: 'The lamp of God had not yet gone out, and Samuel was lying down in the Temple of the LORD, where the ark of God was' (v. 3), we are told. But the peace of Israel's sanctuary is disrupted, at least for the boy at the centre of this tale: 'Then the LORD called, "Samuel! Samuel!" and he said, "Here I am!" and ran to Eli, and said, "Here I am, for you called me." But he said, "I did not call; lie down again." So he went and lay down' (v. 4).

The surprise to the reader lies not in the divine summons, because the author has informed us of who it is that is calling out to Samuel; the shock lies rather in the boy Samuel's mistaken reaction to the divine word. The apparent insider, Samuel, 'in favour with God and with God's people', is unable to discern the source or nature of the word addressed personally to him by the Lord. He is not *inside* the event at all. Instead, Samuel supposes himself summoned to help an old man in the night. Samuel's is an understandable and very reasonable mistake. But it isn't the response of the one we thought was an insider, one who is familiar with the ways of Israel's God. Although God is present and revealing himself to Samuel, nothing happens. This is the shock the story delivers. In fact, this shocking nothing happens three times – just in case we too were inclined to miss the point. It is only on God's *fourth* attempt that Samuel will be ready to read the situation aright.

What helps the author to shock us is the fact that he waits until halfway through his telling of the story to inform us:

'Now Samuel did not yet know the LORD, and the word of the LORD had not yet been revealed to him' (v. 7). This is crucial information, and contrasts sharply with what we had supposed we were being told in the earlier parts of the Samuel story. The narrator has deliberately led us to suppose that the boy Samuel is the religious insider in this story, that he already possesses a hotline to God. If you read around the story, in the earlier and later chapters of 1 Samuel, you will see that the boy Samuel's youthful innocence and obedience, along with the mention of divine favour, is in stark contrast to the outlook and attitudes of the other more senior characters present at the shrine in Shiloh.

So, the story has actually tricked us as we read it – the seeming insider had in fact remained completely an outsider when it comes to the one thing that matters: 'the word of the LORD had not yet been revealed to him'. As we read of the third occasion of God's call, after we have been told the reality of Samuel's situation, suddenly the way we read is different, and we can associate ourselves with Samuel in a way that may not have been true up to this point. With Samuel, we too seek to be 'doers of the word', but perhaps we have not yet fully understood how to become 'hearers of the word'. We are now able to recognize in ourselves the same need that exists in Samuel: as the Ethiopian said, 'How can I, unless someone guides me?'

In Samuel's case, a further twist to the story is the discovery that it is the very inadequate senior priest of the shrine, Eli, who eventually realizes what is really happening to his youthful assistant in the night. The narrator has already told the reader that Eli has lost control of his wayward offspring,

Hophni and Phinehas, and that a severe divine judgement against Eli and his sons is pending. But it nevertheless is Eli, who as the priest of God's shrine represents Israel's memory of everything God has done for his people up to this time, who 'perceived that the LORD was calling the boy' (v. 8): 'Therefore Eli said to Samuel, "Go, lie down; and if he calls you, you shall say, 'Speak, LORD, for your servant is listening.'" So Samuel went and lay down in his place' (v. 9).

The distinction between insider and outsider turns out to be crucial. To whom had Samuel supposed that the story at Shiloh was happening, we might ask? Who were the actors in the drama that was being played out? As the narrative of that momentous night in the Shiloh shrine begins, Samuel still thinks of himself as outside the story; in his own mind he is just a minor player, almost off the stage. As far as Samuel is concerned it is Eli, along with his priest sons Hophni and Phinehas, who are the central characters in the drama of Israel's encounter with the Lord, and it is therefore with and through them that the Lord would speak. What might be termed the 'personal implication' of what is happening – this is you or this is me that this is happening to – has not yet dawned upon the young man. The change that occurs in the course of that night is that the young Samuel discovers, as a consequence of Eli's mentoring, that he is *inside* the story – the events being narrated are happening to him, it is to him that God is speaking.

Now Samuel can appreciate that 'the word of the LORD was addressed to me', as each of Israel's prophets must come to understand. The most basic prerequisite for hearing the voice of the Lord speaking, he has discovered, is that one must allow of the possibility that one might oneself be the person to whom the word is addressed. If any of us begins from the assumption that it is to someone else that these things are happening, that these words are spoken or written, then there is not the slightest possibility that we can hear the Lord speaking. At best, we might simply find ourselves responding to the needs of an old man in the night – doubtless commendable, but less than transformative.

As soon as Samuel enters the story of the night at Shiloh in this personal way (at v. 10), we notice that the way the narrator speaks of the Lord's presence to him is altered – it is as if the reality of the situation has subtly and crucially shifted: 'Now the LORD came and stood there, calling as before, "Samuel! Samuel!"' (v. 10). Even before the boy responds to the call of the Lord, the narrator has told us that Samuel's capacity to grasp what is going on has moved to a different level.

'And Samuel said, "Speak, for your servant is listening." Then the LORD said to Samuel, "See, I am about to do something in Israel that will make both ears of anyone who hears of it tingle"' (vv. 10-11).

In this story we witness the young Samuel learning to discern the voice of the Lord speaking to his prophet. The key to his discernment presented here is found in the moment when, guided by the figure of Eli who represents Israel's history of encounter with its God, Samuel realizes that his people's history is now his own story in the present. No longer is he the outsider looking in as the drama is enacted; he is the insider to whom the story is happening. Just as it did when it was first told, the Samuel story told today can make the ears of its hearers tingle, as we begin to appreciate what is being said.

This is the first shift in perspective needed by the newcomer to prayer with scripture. Like Samuel, or like the Ethiopian official in the book of Acts, we all need guidance on how to find our way into the story of scripture. It is tempting to suppose that it is exclusively knowledge of the history of the text of these ancient documents, awareness of their original language and literary conventions, a sense of the Bible's cultural and historical setting when its books were first written, and a multitude of other valuable more or less specialist elements of knowledge that stand between me as reader and a true encounter with the scriptural text. And it is true that these and other elements of the scripture specialist's expertise are genuinely valuable, and that as our involvement with scripture deepens we will both need and value them more. But the first, and most important, lesson that one who seeks to pray the psalms or read the Bible must learn, whether novice or old hand, is that I am not reading about someone else, long ago and far away. When I seek God in the pages of scripture, God is already seeking me, has indeed already found me, and it is to me that the words I read are addressed.

Samuel's need was to learn how to hear the word of the Lord as addressed to him personally. It is the role of the old priest of Shiloh in this story to communicate to Samuel what Psalm 78 calls the 'things that we have heard and known, that our ancestors have told us' (Ps. 78.3). Eli represents the community that guides us, he is the embodiment of what it means for there to exist a community of faith. We might say that we learn to hear the Lord's voice by listening to the voices of others who are involved in that encounter. It is from our fellow psalm-readers and others who pray with scripture that we catch the capacity to listen to the Lord speaking personally to us.

FINDING THE KEY

One such fellow-reader is Origen of Alexandria, an early third-century Egyptian Christian scholar and teacher of the Bible. One of the Church's greatest ever exponents of how to approach the scriptures as God's word to us, Origen is very far from naive when it comes to understanding the challenge some parts of the scriptures present to readers who are at a distance of time and culture from the circumstances in which the Bible came into being. For all his considerable learning, Origen found that even for him much of scripture was 'filled with riddles, parables, dark sayings, and various other forms of obscurity hard for human nature to comprehend'. It might perhaps offer some reassurance to us moderns that a Christian born so much closer in time to the beginnings of the Church also struggled with parts of the Bible. In Origen's case, this struggle led him to offer us an illuminating parable in one of his commentaries on the Psalms that suggests a way to read scripture fruitfully, helping us to discover a key to the door that can admit us inside the story.

Origen asks us to imagine the Bible as a great mansion with many rooms. We have access to enter this marvellous house but all of its internal rooms, the individual books of scripture, are locked: 'the whole divinely inspired scripture may be likened, because of its obscurity, to many locked rooms in one house', he writes. As Origen develops his image, he suggests that waiting for us outside each room, each book of the Bible, is a key, and each key will open a room in the house – but the key outside any given room is not the one that will admit us to that specific room. Origen writes that 'the keys are scattered about beside the rooms, none of them matching the room by which it is placed'. It can be a difficult task, he says, to find the keys and to match them to the rooms that they can open. Our aim, if we want to get inside the story of scripture, must be to find the right key for the right room.

Origen's point is this: we come to understand each part of scripture only by seeing it in its relationship to the rest of the Bible. As we read, we are assisted by our familiarity with other parts of the Bible, as it is elsewhere in the scriptures that we will find what he calls the 'interpretative principle' to guide us inside the story. Origen's parable of the locked rooms and the keys illuminates the approach Christians have traditionally taken to reading scripture publically in church: passages from different texts are placed beside one another, a reading from the Old Testament preceding a Gospel text, a passage from Paul set against a psalm, so that as each room comes into view an appropriate set of keys can be offered to the explorer. As these texts resonate together in our hearts, each of us who hears them will begin to grasp how the words and motifs from the Old Testament rooms are taken up and spoken afresh in the spaces of the New Testament; also how the gospel message itself throws light back into some of the more curious closets and cupboards of the Old Testament, opening them up to our gaze, so that we gradually become like the wise scribe of Matthew's Gospel, who 'is like the master of a household who brings out of his treasure what is new and what is old' (Mt. 13.52).

Monastic reading, too, strives towards just this end. When I spoke with that novice nun many years ago, this would have been a helpful perspective for us to share together. We might have discovered how the route into Psalm 78 begins within many other books of the scriptural witness; the same wind from God blows elsewhere in the Bible, the fountain flows in many other places, and fire burns to illumine our path throughout both Old and New Testaments. The way that the beginner learns to enter the text, as Origen points out, is exactly the same way that the wise scribe enters the text: by seeking shrewdly among both new and old for the keys that unlock the treasures behind each door.

This is the approach to Lent that I want to share with you in this book. Between the time of that conversation 40 years ago and today, I have gradually learned the rudiments of the art Origen practised with such mastery. To open the many mansions of the scriptures so that they may become places where we find ourselves able to live, to renew our imaginings and empower our actions, monastic reading aims to allow each of us to discover our own keys to the doors of the text. As we read and pray in community, we learn how to step into the diverse rooms of the Bible and to allow the contents of these chambers, furnished in so many distinctive ways, to refurnish the rooms of our own spiritual imaginations.

Such reading is one of the most important ways in which we carry out Saint Paul's injunction: 'be transformed by the renewing of your minds' (Rom. 12.2). As we engage in this undertaking, we begin to find that the Bible is the great reservoir of the Christian imagination, an almost endless resource of possibilities that inspire and renew our faith and allow it to flow into both the imaginative dreamings and the enacted realities of our lives.

THE WIND, THE FOUNTAIN AND THE FIRE

We set out into the many rooms of scripture to be supplied with tools for renewing our minds and hearts in love, in order that we might conform ourselves more closely to the image of Christ. At the same time, our exploration of the scriptures supplies us with a rich fuel that can fire the engines of our endeavour: scripture's poetry enchants and inspires, the Bible gives us the words for our prayers and colourful pictures to inhabit and refresh our imaginations. Biblical narratives and parables offer energy and new perspectives that inspire our hearts. But whether the process of entering the many mansions of the scriptures enables us to discover the tools we can use for our life's task, or helps us to find the fuel that will drive our Christian activity forward, it is in the very language of the Bible that we can claim the most significant of the keys that will actually open up the rooms of scripture for us. The verbal motifs and recurrent language that unify Old and New Testaments, the potent symbols and broad stock of imagery that surrounds each subject the Bible addresses – these are the elements I have found most useful to slip onto my ring of monastic keys as I have begun to wander the halls of the biblical house.

God enjoins upon Old Testament Israel a prohibition of 'graven images', idols or physical representations of the divine (see Exod. 20.4-6). But while painted or sculpted imagery is prohibited, the vivid poetry of biblical language is quite systematically encouraged; this lyrical witness presents us with a sacred kaleidoscope of verbal representations of the Lord God and God's activity in Israel's history. Scripture endlessly calls attention to the power of the word itself, as spoken by a prophet, when sung by a psalmist, or in the preaching of an apostle, to shape our reality by reshaping our minds and hearts. Scripture stirs up our devotion and moves us to activity first and foremost through the force of sacred rhetoric. As the writer to the Hebrews says: 'the word of God is living and active, sharper than any two-edged sword, piercing until it divides soul from spirit, joints from marrow; it is able to judge the thoughts and intentions of the heart' (Heb. 4.12).

The sharp and piercing language of the Bible actively 'images' its subjects; it paints pictures of the points it wishes to make, much more often than it simply states them. And so Paul instructs the church in Colossae: 'Let the word of Christ dwell in you richly; teach and admonish one another in all wisdom; and with gratitude in your hearts sing psalms, hymns, and spiritual songs to God' (Col. 3.16). Approaching scripture through the songs of the psalmist, the hymnology of Paul, or the pictures painted by prophets and evangelists is among the most fruitful methods for opening some of the doors that we encounter within Origen's house of locked rooms, for finding routes for ourselves into the inside of the story.

My aim in *The Wind, the Fountain and the Fire* is to do just this, to take up the imagery of scripture as the key for an exploration of the biblical themes of Lent. Each of the five chapters that follows arises from a reflection upon a single scriptural motif or image, one for each of the five great Sundays of the Lenten season that lead us into Passiontide and Holy Week. Each image is drawn from the Gospel text we read together in church on the successive Sundays of Lent, and each image brings us into contact with a wide range of scriptural texts: from the psalms, from elsewhere in the Gospels, and from across the whole biblical witness from Genesis to Revelation. The keys towards which Origen directs us are to be found by placing scriptural texts alongside one another and by noticing how these texts make use of repeated motifs and images to resonate in our minds and enable us to see, hear, taste and touch salvation. As the psalmist writes of those who take refuge in the shelter of God's wings:

> They feast on the abundance of your house,
> and you give them drink from the river of your delights.
> For with you is the fountain of life;
> in your light we see light.
>
> (Ps. 36.8-9)

I began the introduction to this book with the tale of my failure adequately to articulate the business of praying the psalms when I was asked a question about Psalm 78, noticing that one way I might have begun to think about this poem – but had not then considered – was to engage imaginatively with the psalmist's imagery of gusting wind, flowing fountain and fiery light, the rich pattern of literary motifs that are scattered so generously across the length of that psalm's text. Let me conclude by setting alongside my personal story of failure a much more significant, biblical tale – that of the prophet Elijah at Mount Sinai, as told in 1 Kings 19. This story, too, involves a failure, as we shall see. A failure that has much to teach us.

Elijah's story is set in the ninth century BCE, during the period of biblical history usually called the 'divided kingdom'. The two books of Kings recount a period after the reigns of David and his son Solomon over a unified Israelite nation of roughly two hundred years during which there were two separate Hebrew kingdoms: Israel in the north, and Judah in the south. This period would end in the tragedy of exile and the successive destruction of both Israelite nations.

The part of the Elijah story I want to consider comes towards the end of the prophet's work in the northern kingdom of Israel. The king of Israel, Ahab, has thrown in his lot with the religious outlook of his Phoenician wife, Jezebel, who worships the deities of her native Sidon, a port city very different from landlocked Israel. It has been Elijah's life-threatening mission to stand against the idolatry the royal couple both practise. In a tumultuous confrontation with the idol worshippers at Mt Carmel, Elijah has sought to strike a decisive blow against Israel's apostasy – but the cost to him is high: the malevolent power of the royal court is turned directly upon him, and he flees for his life, pursued by the threat of death. In Elijah's own words: 'I have been very

zealous for the LORD, the God of hosts; for the Israelites have
forsaken your covenant, thrown down your altars, and killed
your prophets with the sword. I alone am left, and they are
seeking my life, to take it away' (1 Kgs 19.10).

In his terror, Elijah takes refuge in the deserts to the
south of Israel and Judah, spending many weeks crossing
the barren lands to arrive at the mountain of God, Sinai, [1]
cared for on the way by angels sent to him with food and
water. In the book of Exodus, Sinai is the place where God
gave the law to Moses, thereby establishing the covenant
relationship that Elijah has sought to defend. It is as if Elijah
has pilgrimaged back to the very starting point of the faith
in Israel's God to which he holds firm and which he has
worked to promote; it may even seem that he no longer
believes the promised land of Canaan can be safe for those
who worship the God of Israel, and that the whole enterprise
of establishing a kingdom and a nation is unravelling. Elijah's
terror in the face of the royal fury unleashed against him is
entirely justified, but what happens next suggests that his
reaction to that terror is not the one that the God of Israel
had called for. On Sinai, God judges Elijah's flight in an
unexpected way.

It is when Elijah reaches the mountain of God, spending the
night in a cave on the mountainside, that God asks him: 'What
are you doing here, Elijah?' (v. 9). The prophet replies in the
words mentioned earlier, speaking of his zeal, the Israelites'
infidelity, and his fear for his life: 'I alone am left'.

---

[1] The Bible uses two different names for this mountain: it is known both as 'Horeb' and as 'Sinai'. To avoid confusion, I will always refer simply to Sinai.

Now comes one of the most extraordinary passages in all
the prophetic literature of the Old Testament. Elijah is told
to leave the cave, and go out onto the mountain, for God is
about to pass by. There is in this text more than an echo of the
awe-inspiring moment in the book of Exodus when the Lord
passes by Moses on the same mountain, a moment of gracious
intimacy in which God speaks his own name to his chosen
messenger (see Exod. 34). This echo is surely intentional. In
the Elijah story there follows a series of three violent natural
phenomena – wind, earthquake and fire – again reminiscent
of the Exodus narrative. Each one of these signs occurs
frequently in the Old Testament to indicate a 'theophany', a
moment when God is present; these signs usually mean that
the creator has stepped into his creation.

First there occurs a great wind so strong that it threatens
to split the very mountain, 'but the LORD was not in the
wind' (1 Kgs 19.11), we are told. After the wind comes
an earthquake, the shattering of the ground and the rocks
on the mountain, but once again 'the LORD was not in the
earthquake' (v. 11). And finally, to complete the full set of
three empty signs, after the earthquake there follows a fire,
and once more 'the LORD was not in the fire' (v. 12).

The story of Elijah on the mountain has become quite well
known, and this can prevent us from recognizing its force.
You and I probably don't expect God to be manifested in the
wind, the shattered rocks, or the fire, partly because this story
says that he wasn't. I have heard this passage misunderstood
more than once as some kind of disavowal by scripture of
so-called 'primitive' concepts of God, written to tell us that
God no longer makes himself present in such melodramatic

ways as wind, earthquake or fire. I don't read it that way,
and I don't think it is written that way either. Usually,
misunderstandings of this story begin with a mistranslation
of the statement that comes immediately after the account
of the empty signs: 'after the fire a sound of sheer silence'
(v. 12). The story is not contrasting the Wagnerian tantrum
on the mountain, which does not manifest God, with the
gentle voice of sweet reason in which God is present, the 'still
small voice' of the King James Bible translation of this verse.
That venerable translation is rich in evocative poetry, but
here it misunderstands a Hebrew idiom, with unfortunate
consequences. What the text boldly and clearly says is that
God is absent – not in the wind, not in the earthquake, not
in the fire – and silent.

To help us better appreciate the force of the three
non-signs and the silence presented to Elijah, let me
point to the example of Psalm 18. Like Elijah on Sinai,
the psalmist here is in fear for his life: 'The cords of death
encompassed me ... the snares of death confronted me'
(Ps. 18.4-5). He tells us that 'in my distress I called upon
the LORD ... and my cry to him reached his ears' (vv. 6-7).
There follows the large-scale display of divine pyrotechnics
that frequently appears in the Old Testament to signal
God's saving presence, in which God acts to deliver his
endangered servant. The psalmist tells of earthquake, fire
and wind:

Then the earth reeled and rocked;
the foundations also of the mountains trembled
and quaked, because he was angry.

Smoke went up from his nostrils,
and devouring fire from his mouth;
glowing coals flamed forth from him.
He bowed the heavens, and came down;
thick darkness was under his feet.
He rode on a cherub, and flew;
he came swiftly upon the wings of the wind.

(Ps. 18.7-10)

This set of signs specifically indicates that God is present to reach down and save the one in need 'from my strong enemy, and from those who hated me' (v. 17).

It is just such an event that the Elijah story narrates, but the central character, God, is missing. Elijah stands on the mountain where his prophetic predecessor, Moses, received the law from God, but whereas in the exodus Moses experienced the wind from God that blew strongly across the Red Sea to part the waters and set God's people free, on Sinai Elijah simply experiences a gale. For Moses as he led Israel through the desert and was in need of water to drink, the smashing of the desert rocks in an earthquake brought forth fountains of fresh water in the wilderness, delivering Israel from death and manifesting God's steadfast love; on Sinai, Elijah only witnesses nature smashing against itself in empty violence. When the bush was enveloped with flames of fire before Moses, and yet not consumed, it signalled the intervention of Israel's God, fiery at the injustice suffered by his people; on Sinai, Elijah sees only a bush fire. And then in 'the sound of sheer silence', Elijah experiences what the prophet Amos will later call 'a famine of the word of God' (see Amos 8.11). Instead of God's presence and God's word spoken, Elijah is plunged into an experience of God's absence and silence.

'What are you doing here, Elijah?' God asks of him twice on the mountain. The two questions form an *inclusio* (they come before and after the story, like a pair of bookends), a literary device sometimes employed to frame a story and point towards its significance. Here they give the clue as to why Elijah's visit to Sinai has such strange consequences. The prophet's flight to Sinai is an act of judgement he has passed in terrified panic and in haste on the people of Israel, who he says have forsaken God's covenant, thrown down his altars and killed his prophets. By returning to the holy mountain, it is as if Elijah symbolically seeks to undo the journey Israel undertook first with Moses and then with Joshua into the promised land. He seems to cast aside any possibility that there might still be faith in God to be found among his people: 'I am the only one left,' he says. It is as if Elijah, in his desperation, seeks to step out of the story that God has been shaping with his chosen people. He has fled away from what God is doing in Israel every bit as much as the prophet Jonah fled from God's instruction to preach in Nineveh. If it is true that Elijah in his terror has stepped out of Israel's saving encounter with its God, then this is why the saving signs on the mountain are empty, why the word that follows them is silent.

And what this means is that God very clearly rejects Elijah's judgement on Israel – after twice asking him why he has done what he has done, after showing him in vivid signs that the God of Israel will not step into the creation to undo his own saving justice, God very bluntly turns Elijah around and sends him back the way he has come: 'Then the LORD said to him, "Go, return on your way to the wilderness of Damascus …"' (1 Kgs 19.15). Elijah is, effectively, given very direct instructions on how to re-join the story of what God is working in Israel: the list of violent international political coups that Elijah is then instructed to initiate gives the lie to the view that a still small voice whispering words of peace was the intended meaning of the Sinai story. This story is rather one of how the word is deeply strange, discomforting and even threatening. Like his ancestor Abraham, Elijah is told: get up and go where I shall send you.

In this strange story of absence and silence there is a parable of where many of us begin the season of Lent. Our beginning is a place not so very different from where we found Elijah, though in our case that place is perhaps painted in somewhat less lurid colours. You or I are unlikely to have been called upon to fight publically to defend true religion against a state that seeks to assail God's values. But we do live in a context where Christian faith is more or less subtly marginalized on a daily basis, and we may find our own faith eroded and diminished in our regular exposure to these everyday encounters. Too often tepid in our own commitment, we may begin to lose hope, we can come to believe that earlier effort has been in vain. We lose sight of our original vision of where Christ is leading us. Lent finds us as people who have begun the process of slipping out of the story, once more imagining ourselves back somewhere on the sidelines with no role to play as God's drama of salvation unfolds into other people's futures. The call to step back into the story God is trying to tell us is the opportunity Lent places before us. Saint Paul's words are addressed to each of us: 'be transformed by the renewing of your minds' (Rom. 12.2). The path through Lent begins in the rooms of our imaginations.

In the empty signs Elijah encounters on Sinai – the wind, the earthquake and the fire – are to be found anticipatory glimpses of where every Lenten journey is intended by God to take us. If we hear and answer the call of Lent, if we travel in the strength of that call for 40 days and 40 nights, we will arrive at the Easter mountain of the crucifixion and resurrection. Here we may gaze up to discover, in the mystery of Pentecost, that the great wind now blows to bring the Spirit of God back into our lives: 'suddenly from heaven there came a sound like the rush of a violent wind' (Acts 2.2); that the stony hearts with which we began the season break open through the fountains of baptism, 'Repent, and be baptized every one of you in the name of Jesus Christ' (v. 38); and that a blazing fire can still inflame our imaginations and our actions, 'Divided tongues, as of fire, appeared among them, and a tongue rested on each of them' (v. 3). The wind, the fountain and the fire are the signs of God's Pentecostal promise of the renewed minds and hearts he wishes to bestow upon us all as we re-enter the scriptural story he is telling of a world transformed in Jesus Christ.

In the book of Acts, where the story of Pentecost is recounted, Peter preaches to the first ever converts to the Christian faith, quoting from the Old Testament prophet, Joel:

In the last days it will be, God declares,
that I will pour out my Spirit upon all flesh,

and your sons and your daughters shall prophesy,
and your young men shall see visions,
and your old men shall dream dreams.

(Acts 2.17)

It is not only in the 'last days' that the Spirit of God will empower us to see visions and dream dreams. This same gift is offered by God's Holy Spirit to us today, to renew our Christian imaginations in Lent.

The Dust: Ash Wednesday and the First Week of Lent

Then Jesus was led up by the Spirit into the wilderness to be tempted by the devil. (Matthew 4:1)

It all begins with dust.

Dirty dust is the sign that opens Lent in our Ash Wednesday liturgies, and we all emerge from church with this sign prominently placed on our foreheads: 'Remember that you are dust, and to dust you shall return,' says the priest to each of us. Just a few days later, the sequence of Lent's five Sundays opens our scriptural journey, with Matthew's account of the temptations in the desert (Mt. 4.1-11). We hear of how Jesus begins his teaching ministry by responding to John the Baptist's call: he ventures into the arid dust of the desert lands, 'into the wilderness to be tempted by the devil'. The starting point of Lent for all of us is very clear. We begin from the place this dust positions us in: we 'repent in dust and ashes' (Job 42.6).

To repent, to be converted, is to involve ourselves in a lifelong process of personal change, a renewal affecting every dimension of ourselves and our activities. And just

as each of us knows this as we begin Lent, we also know
only too well how difficult we find the reality that follows
uncomfortably close behind the theory. Even more than is
the case with our secular New Year resolutions, now almost
proverbial for the frequency and ease with which they
are abandoned, there is a deep-seated reluctance in us to
respond to God's Lenten call, a *not wanting* rather than an
eagerness; Ash Wednesday is well named for those of us who
find our hearts dry as dust when the holy season of Lent
comes around.

I'd like to suggest that we pay some attention to that
dryness. Instead of trying to rub the dust from our hearts
as superficially and as quickly as I fear I have sometimes
rubbed the ashes from my forehead as I emerged from
the Lenten liturgy, perhaps the desiccation we discover
within ourselves offers an unexpected doorway into
the truth of Lent. The biblical narrative helps us here.
Scripture employs the image of the dry dust beneath our
feet in two radically different ways – both as a negative and
as a positive. As we are 'dusted' for the beginning of the
Lenten season, we should notice both its facets in order to
appreciate what is happening in the ceremony of ashes – as
well as what it might mean to recognize the ashen state of
our hearts.

It is most likely to be the unfavourable meanings of dust
that we are thinking about as we approach Ash Wednesday. We
see these connotations at work when the psalmist complains
that he is laid in the 'dust of death' (Ps. 22.15), or is sinking
'down to the dust' (Ps. 44.25); it is easy to grasp that this
is the imagery of desolation or diminishment, of a decline

towards death. 'My soul clings to the dust' (Ps. 119.25), the psalmist cries out, recalling the life-giving strength that has slipped away from him. On a larger scale, towards the end of the book of Deuteronomy the wilderness of dust and ashes through which Israel journeys is characterized as a 'howling wilderness waste' (Deut. 32.10); in such a death-dealing space, only the direct intervention of God can preserve life. All of these are negative images of the 'dust to which we shall return'; this first meaning of dust as death or diminishment is regularly to be discovered throughout the Bible.

But scripture just as regularly invokes a second and far more positive signification of this unpromising earth-stuff. Recognizing this adds a wholly different, transformative dimension to the Ash Wednesday celebration. 'The LORD God formed man from the dust of the ground', the book of Genesis tells us (Gen. 2.7): the dust of the earth is the crucial raw material from which all human life is fashioned and gifted by a loving creator with the breath of life. Humanity is constituted as dust beloved by the Lord. Dust is the most basic, necessary stuff of human life as fashioned by God, even while it simultaneously represents the ephemeral nature of that life. Thus, even as the suffering Job complains that his life is so diminished as to be turned back to dust again, he cries out to the faithful God who 'fashioned me like clay' (Job 10.9), the creator who made a living thing from the earth underfoot. Humanity's shame is, in a paradoxical simultaneity, the ground – quite literally – of our claim upon God.

Looking more widely across scripture, we find that dust is the image used positively to denote fecundity and

prosperity in the book of Genesis as Jacob dreams of the
ladder at Bethel, a dream in which a divine blessing is
pronounced – through this same dust – upon all life: 'your
offspring', Jacob is told, 'shall be like the dust of the earth ...
and all the families of the earth shall be blessed in you and
in your offspring' (Gen. 28.14). And when the prophets,
speaking in the name of God, promise a future of hope to
God's people beyond the tribulations of the present, it is to
the apparently unpromising landscape of the wilderness of
dust, the desert, that they are drawn. Throughout the later
chapters of Isaiah, for example, the howling wilderness
waste becomes the gateway to fresh, new hope: 'I will make a
way in the wilderness, and rivers in the desert', the prophet
proclaims in God's name (Isa. 43.19); the image is that of
a triumphant path of life for God and his people through
the desolate landscape, which blossoms with new fertility in
response to their arrival.

As Lent begins, this double sign of dust – the dust
descending to death and the dust from which abundant new
life is called forth – features prominently both in the Lenten
liturgy and in the scriptural witness. To 'remember that
you are dust, and to dust you shall return' is to acknowledge
sin and failure, to recognize the dust of death at work in
our lives; it is also to embrace the hope of resurrection,
joyfully to anticipate the day of the Lord's promise to
raise us up 'from the dust ... and inherit a seat of honour'
(1 Sam. 2.8).

In a story unique to the Fourth Gospel, we read in John
8 of how Jesus is confronted with those who wish him to
rush to judgement against one they believe to be a sinner,

an alleged adulteress (see Jn 8.1-11). We are told of Jesus' unanticipated response to this challenge. Jesus leaves the woman able to go on her way, and presents her with what is effectively the same injunction issued to each of us as Lent begins: 'Turn away from sin, and believe the good news.' A tantalizing detail of the story is the way Jesus is pictured as reacting to the accusers' insistent demand for a judgement against the woman: 'Jesus bent down and wrote with his finger on the ground' (Jn 8.6). Everyone who reads this story is, inevitably, left wondering what Jesus was writing in the dust. Some early manuscripts of this part of the Gospel text even appear to offer evidence of scribes attempting to supply answers to that question on their readers' behalf, beginning to fill in the blanks of the narrative with new portions of text. But the reality is that, like the white stones in the book of Revelation on which are written the secret names belonging to each of us, what Jesus wrote in the dust 'no one knows except the one who receives it' (Rev. 2.17). Each of us must look into the dust of his or her own life, to read what the Lord is writing there.

In this first chapter, I want to pause on the threshold of Lent to discover more of what it may be that the Lord is writing today in that dry dust, in the ashes of our hearts.

REMEMBER THAT YOU ARE DUST

Psalm 90, a prayer in which the psalmist cries out to God in the name of his whole people for help in time of difficulty, opens with a stark contrast between the mountainous eternity of God, the sure refuge, for whom a thousand years pass like

a watch in the night, and the fleeting brevity of human life,
brief as the existence of the morning's grass that withers into
dust by nightfall:

> You turn us back to dust,
> and say, 'Turn back, you mortals.'
>
> (Ps. 90. 3)

The psalmist appeals to the steadfast God who is the sure
refuge of his people to 'teach us to count our days, that we
may gain a wise heart' (Ps. 90.12). This is the wisdom of
humility before the majesty of God, certainly, but it is also
the wisdom that places its hope in the divine fidelity, rather
than in some illusory personal strength. The psalm finds in
the remembrance that human beings come from the dust and
shall return to it the occasion for a renewed hope in the God
of Israel, who turns back to his suffering people to give joy in
place of affliction, so that 'we may rejoice and be glad all our
days' (Ps. 90.14).

As we get to know the psalms, we discover that they
regularly manifest a paradoxical ground for confident faith
in this frank acknowledgement of human evanescence: it is
the fleeting nature of human existence that entitles us to call
out for the help of God. In Psalm 103, for example, we find
the same viewpoint as that of Psalm 90: 'As for mortals, their
days are like grass ... the wind passes over it, and it is gone,
and its place knows it no more' (Ps. 103.15-16). The life of
each of us will end in the dust from which we came. But for
the psalmist it is this very fact of our coming from the dust
that inspires divine compassion:

As a father has compassion for his children,
so the LORD has compassion for those who fear him.
For he knows how we were made;
he remembers that we are dust.

(Ps. 103.13-14)

Fully to appreciate what this psalm is saying, we need to look a little more closely at the claim that God 'remembers' that we are dust.

When you or I say that we 'remember' this or that, we may perhaps congratulate ourselves on our cleverness, our breadth of learning or our powers of recall. Essentially, for us these words describe an intellectual act. But for God to 'remember' never suggests, for the psalmist or for scripture more generally, that the Lord merely has access to a wide range of facts together with the intellectual bandwidth consciously to juggle them all at the same time.

God's remembering is more viscerally self-implicating. 'I have inscribed you on the palms of my hands' (Isa. 49.16), the prophet Isaiah has God say of God's remembering of his people. 'Can a woman forget her nursing-child', Isaiah asks, 'or show no compassion for the child of her womb?' (Isa. 49.15). The rhetorical question points out that for God to 'remember' (in Hebrew this verb signifies remembering as an activity that is personal and relational) is for God to act towards humanity out of his very nature as 'a God merciful and gracious, slow to anger and abounding in steadfast love and graciousness' (Exod. 34.6). In scripture, God's remembering of his people is always a personally motivated, saving action. The psalmist thinks of God's remembering as his very activity of being the God of Israel, the saviour. For God to remember is for God to save.

When we are dusted with ashes for the beginning of Lent and hear the words 'Remember that you are dust', we are being enjoined to do something more than simply have in mind our sinfulness, to recall the story of the garden of Eden in Genesis 3 where it all went wrong. To 'remember that we are dust' is also to look back to what has happened just before the story of the fall of Adam and Eve, namely the Genesis chapter 2 narrative of the making of the *adam* (humanity) from the *adamah* (the red earth of the desert). Our Lenten encounter with dust invites us to return to the biblical account of that foundational moment when God first creates the human person.

The awe-inspiring creation narrative of Genesis 1, 'In the beginning when God created the heavens and the earth …', liturgical in structure and dramatically re-presented frequently in the art and music of Western culture, is so powerful a piece of writing that it has seized for itself the high ground of the Christian imagination as if it were the one and only creation story in the Bible. Even so, most readers of the Bible have become used to the fact that the creation story of Genesis 2 comes most probably from an account older than that of chapter 1; the two accounts have been united by the redactors of the Genesis material.

'In the day that the LORD God made the earth and heavens', the book of Genesis tells us as the chapter 2 creation story opens, when there were neither plants nor herbs and the first rains had yet to fall from a young sky upon the reddish earth of a shapeless wilderness, 'then the LORD God formed

man from the dust of the ground' (Gen. 2.4, 7). You could
not ask for a more foundational happening than this. The
biblical narrative of this moment locates God's choice to
call into life those who can bear God's own image and
likeness in the dust of a desert wasteland; the unpromising
raw material chosen by God for this action is dust from the
wide waste ground.

As this version of the creation narrative begins, the author
invites us to notice the one distinguishing feature of an
otherwise uniformly arid wasteland: a place where 'a stream
would rise from the earth, and water the whole face of the
ground' (Gen. 2.6). It will be here, at this very spot, that
the Lord God will soon plant the garden known as Eden; it
is 'in the east', and here God will make to grow 'every tree
that is pleasant to the sight and good for food' (v. 9). But
on the day our human story begins, 'the day that the LORD
God made the earth and heavens' (v. 4), the moment just
before there is an *adam*, a human person, this *adamah*, this
red earth, remains 'a desert land ... a howling wilderness
waste' (Deut. 32.10).

As we read Genesis 2 we can watch in our imagination
as the Lord God stoops to the ground, kneeling down into
the dust, beside the stream that is rising there. The God
'who made the Pleiades and Orion, and turns deep darkness
into the morning, and darkens the day into night, who calls
for the waters of the sea, and pours them out on the surface
of the earth' (Amos 5.8) reaches down to the earth beneath
his feet, grasps lumps from the red dust in his hands, gently
kneads it with some water from the stream until his arms
are elbow deep in moist red clay, and 'forms' (the Hebrew

word here means physically grabbing and shaping, to squeeze, like a potter with the clay of a vessel); the Lord God forms, shapes, squeezes the clay of the human person from the dust of the waste ground mixed with the water of the stream.

And God, we are told, 'breathed into his nostrils the breath of life; and the man became a living being' (Gen. 2.7). The *adamah* has been transformed; the *adam* has come to be. The human person is made of moistened wilderness and of the divine wind, of wet dust and God's very breath. Psalm 8, a hymn that meditates on the marvels of God's creation, shares the sense of awe evoked by the Genesis author's stark juxtaposition of God's sublime ordering of a cosmos in chapter 1 and this direct hands-on shaping of the human person in chapter 2:

When I look at your heavens, the work of your fingers,
the moon and the stars that you have established;
what are human beings that you are mindful of them,
mortals that you care for them?

(Psalm 8.3-4)

The moment of the creation of humanity, pictured so physically by the Genesis author, is sculpturally rendered in a most remarkable image found in one of the bays in Chartres Cathedral's North Porch. Here, a thirteenth-century sculptor, every bit as anonymous as the Genesis author, depicts the Lord God as a handsome young man, bearded and with a flowing head of hair, his features echoing those often associated with

Christ in Western art. The creator God is seated, gently supporting the figure of a newly formed Adam upon his lap, the creator's hands still working around the head and face of his adult new-born, who reaches out to clasp the knees of his maker. The creator's gaze, like the action of his hands, is focused upon this new human, whose head is resting upon the creator's chest – it seems the new-born has yet fully to awake.

This sculpture is a realization in pictorial form of the event told of with succinct power in the Genesis narrative. I am especially struck by the Chartres craftsman's desire to portray the human person so immediately as the work of God's hands, and the corresponding interest we see in his work to portray the human hand reaching out to touch the divine.

The second-century bishop and theologian, Irenaeus of Lyons, understands the divine work of fashioning humanity in a manner that casts light upon both the Chartres sculpture and the biblical story it depicts. 'You are God's workmanship; you should await the hand of your maker which creates everything in due time ... you whose creation is being carried out', writes Irenaeus in his book called *Against the Heresies*. The work of God in his human creation is understood by Irenaeus as very far from finished. The hand of the maker, he suggests, is still working in us, we whose creation is still being carried out.

Irenaeus goes on to invite all God's human creatures to offer our hearts to him 'in a soft and tractable state, and preserve the form in which the creator has fashioned you, having moisture in yourself'. If we humans lose the moisture of divine grace, Irenaeus says, we not only become simply hardened clay, we also 'lose the impressions of his fingers', we cease to respond to the creator. If we are willing to remain God's work-in-progress, Irenaeus suggests, we shall 'ascend to that which is perfect, for the moist clay which is in you is hidden there by the workmanship of God'.

For Irenaeus, the *adam* formed from the *adamah*, the new-born human of the Chartres sculpture, remains crucially unfinished. The Lord God is holding this moist clay, and continues to fashion his human children; 'for never at any time did Adam escape the hands of God'. The divine potter never lifts his hands from the vessel. 'His hands formed a living man, in order that Adam might be created again after the image and likeness of God.'

It is tempting to suppose that the anonymous medieval artist of the Chartres North Porch might have had Irenaeus' words in mind as he created the beautiful images of his creation sequence. Of the several panels of the creation sequence at Chartres, it is only here, in this single image of the creation of humanity, that the creator is depicted as making physical contact with his creation – elsewhere, the world and all it contains appear in response to the creator's gestures. Uniquely with the human he fashions, God is here shown working by hand. And, in the stone of Chartres, as in Irenaeus' prose, never at any time does the human person escape the hands of God. Adam reclines against the knee of his maker, as God's hand touches the moist clay hidden within the stone.

The forming of humanity from the clay, and God's continued nurturing involvement with his beloved children, is an emphatic statement that God is communicating himself to humanity constantly. This is what it means for us to be God's creation. The human person is constituted as one who is gifted by God with the capacity to be in communion with God; it cannot happen that there is a human life in which the creator is not intimately involved. To 'remember that you are dust' is to remember this fundamental reality. Even as these words remind us that death is our universal destiny, they simultaneously call us to awaken to a recognition of our foundational relationship with God as our source and centre. In the short and hauntingly beautiful poetry of Psalm 131, the psalmist positions the human person before God as the child, newly weaned, sleeping peacefully on the lap of its mother: 'I have calmed and quieted my soul, like a weaned child with its mother' (Ps. 131.2). Psalm 131 is the prayer that might surface within our soul as we contemplate the astonishing truth of who we are, as human creatures, in the hands of God.

In the psalms this fundamental and continuing relationship between the creator and his human creatures, we 'whose creation is being carried out', is nowhere more explicitly explored than in Psalm 139. In the context of Ash Wednesday, we tend to focus on psalms that express sorrow for sin, and the penitence that rightly characterizes the Lenten season. Psalm 139, 'O LORD, you have searched me and known me', invites us to understand that the dryness and hardness of heart we experience, the dust of our nature, is known well and encompassed in love by the creator God, who works constantly to make a human person from this unpromising material: for the glory of God is a living person, and the life

of a human person comes from the vision of God, as Irenaeus
of Lyons also wrote.

Psalm 139 is an intensely personal confession of faith by the
psalmist in Israel's steadfast God. In a language of intimacy
and an imagery of God's ceaseless activity in his human
creation, we are asked to join the psalmist in recognizing
the deep relatedness not only of God and his chosen people,
but very specifically the individual relationship of creature
and creator, in fact my own relationship with God. This
psalm asks me to understand myself to be the *adam* we have
watched as God shaped humanity from the *adamah*, the
earth dust, and to realize that 'it was you who formed my
inward parts; you knit me together in my mother's womb'
(Ps. 139.13).

The psalm begins its celebration of God's closeness to us
in verses 1-6 by detailing the Lord's complete knowledge of
the actions, words, thoughts of each one of us. If we have in
mind that this 'wonderful' knowledge is not that of a system
of surveillance but rather the saving and loving involvement
of the creator who wishes to give life, we shall read aright:

O LORD, you have searched me and known me.
You know when I sit down and when I rise up;
you discern my thoughts from far away.

(Ps. 139.1-2)

The psalmist confesses that 'such knowledge is too wonderful
for me; it is so high that I cannot attain it' (Ps. 139.6),
marvelling at the divine humility that can attend even to the
smallest concern of God's creatures and also recognizing in

wonder that the creator is closer to our secret self than we ourselves might be.

There is something in each of us, I suspect, that recognizes an unknown aspect to ourselves, something not accessible even to our closest friends and intimates, and perhaps in some sense not fully grasped even by ourself. The psalmist recognizes this dimension in himself, and also knows that the creator, the 'judge of all the earth' (Gen. 18.25), who knows his creation's words before we speak them, is very close to this partly known, deep self. The image of God as judge is often understood as threatening and can at worst induce that rigidity of outlook and scrupulous concern for legalized morality that Jesus found in the religious leaders of his own day. But perhaps a better way to think of the judgement of God is to understand, as the psalmist seems to recognize, that only the one whose 'eyes beheld my unformed substance' (Ps. 139.16) really knows me through and through. Here is one who truly knows who I am, and who – if I will allow this – is always at hand to help me to know this too.

The second part of the psalm, verses 7-12, pictures the universal presence of God's love in our lives. The psalmist rhetorically inquires, 'Where can I flee from your presence?' (v. 7), before listing a series of far-off or unreachable places into which the love of God can effortlessly penetrate: wherever we are, in all circumstances, the Lord's 'right hand shall hold me fast' (Ps. 139.10). This theme of the Lord's closeness is explored in an imagery of height and depth, of darkness and light. The psalmist anticipates Saint Paul's ecstatic cry in his letter to the Romans: 'Who will separate us from the love of Christ? ... For I am convinced that neither death, nor life, nor angels, nor rulers, nor things present, nor things to come, nor powers, nor height, nor depth, nor anything else in all creation, will be able to separate us from the love of God in Christ Jesus our Lord' (Rom. 8.35, 38-39). As Jesus will say in Saint Luke's Gospel, we are not to fear separation from the loving creator; it is God's 'good pleasure' to involve himself in the details of our everyday (see Lk. 12.22-32). For the psalmist too, there is nowhere I can go and nothing that I can do that will hide me from God's transforming, supporting love.

Verses 13-18, the third section of this psalm, move our consideration from the heights and depths of the creator's love, to search in our physical origins for further praise of Israel's God: 'I praise you, for I am fearfully and wonderfully made' (v. 14). The psalmist first speaks of the marvel of God's activity in knitting the human person together in the womb. His awe is evoked not only by the biological marvel of human life, but also by the perspective articulated in the words of the prophet Jeremiah at the beginning of his ministry to Israel: 'Before I formed you in the womb I knew you, and before you were born I consecrated you' (Jer. 1.5). This is the same perspective we meet in the first chapter of Saint Luke's Gospel, as the expectant mothers Elizabeth and Mary each recognize in her own way that the child she is carrying is already known by God as he grows in her womb. In Psalm 139 the psalmist goes on to associate our conception and gestation in the womb with God's creation of the first human person, in Genesis, as the psalm ponders the process whereby each of us is 'intricately woven in the depths of the earth', an image that looks towards the forming of the *adam* from the dust of the earth in the garden of God. Looking forward through the life of each of us, the psalmist in verse 16 imagines God's providential care and continuing involvement in the shaping of our destiny through the image of a book in which all our days are written when none of them as yet existed.

The fourth and final part of this moving mediation on the love of the creator, verses 19-24, usually comes as a profound shock to the modern reader. The psalmist seems to shift gear completely, and utters a series of urgent pleas to God for the death of the wicked, those who murder believers and threaten God's faithful:

> Do I not hate those who hate you, O Lord?
> And do I not loathe those who rise up against you?
>
> (Ps. 139.21)

So abrupt, so complete is the change of tone in these so-called cursing verses that in many contexts they are regularly omitted from the psalm. For a period of years my own monastery did exactly this. Today, we have – I think rightly – restored the integrity of God's word, and we sing the psalm in its entirety. There are a number of passages elsewhere in the psalms that display a similar set of attitudes. The restoration of the cursing verses in any context of worship forces on us the question of how to understand them, and how it might be possible to pray them.

The first, and perhaps the most important, point of which we need to be aware is the way that the psalmist, in common with many biblical writers, does not usually distinguish between a set of activities and the outlook that goes with them, on the one hand, and the people who carry out these activities, on the other. So when, for example, the psalmist seeks to condemn unjust actions and exploitation, lies about God, or the oppression of those who are defenceless, and prays to God for an end to such abuses of his human creatures, it is those who carry out the actions against whom the psalm prayer is directed: the wicked action is condemned in the persons of 'the wicked'. In praying against 'the wicked' we pray for an end to evil, injustice and oppression in God's world. We pray for the death of every human outlook and attitude that condones and enables such evil to exist, whether in ourselves or in others.

The second issue to have in mind is that, in practice, we ourselves do not always succeed in making the neat moral distinction I have just outlined between evil and the evildoer when we encounter real-life situations of hurt, malice, exploitation or crime. I know that as a Christian I am called to love the sinner while hating the sin, and to forgive wrongs done to me, but I doubt any of us finds this an immediate and straightforward response when we stumble into situations where real evil is at work. The psalmist's frankly murderous reaction to the out-workings of sin in the world is alive and well in our own hearts also, and we do well to be aware of this. Part of the function of the cursing verses in the psalms for Christians who find themselves able to pray them is to enable us to notice the murder that is in our own hearts, and to place it before the Lord in prayer.

Psalm 139, then, seeks to shape our hearts and imaginations in several ways. As we 'remember that we are dust' on the threshold of Lent, this psalm prayer pictures God at work in the life of each individual believer; the psalm allows us to understand ourselves as placed in the same relationship with the loving God as Adam at the knees of Christ in the Chartres sculpture. The dust of our hearts is taken up by the gracious creator and moistened by the love and continuing involvement of God, so that we may continue to be shaped into his image. We are made of wilderness-stuff – in order that in us the desert can blossom; but, as the final section of the psalm reminds us, we also have it in our power to return to the howling waste that can devour and destroy. To turn away from sin on Ash Wednesday is to turn back from this murderous waste-place, acknowledging before God that it still grips us even to the core of our being, and to ask God to moisten it, to pummel it, shaping and shifting our thoughts, our feelings and our actions, until we can truly believe the good news of his Son.

THE TEMPTATIONS IN THE DESERT

On the first Sunday of Lent, we read the story of the temptation of Jesus in the wilderness (Mt. 4.1-11). This Gospel narrative can be a story we admire from afar rather than becoming an event that we feel we are involved in at any personal level. But Matthew's Gospel helps us by directing our attention back to the stories recounted in the books that follow Genesis in the Old Testament, in which God begins the lengthy struggle to form a holy people; another divine work that commences in a wilderness of dust. Israel's wilderness journey that follows the exodus from Egypt forms the subject of most of the rest of the Pentateuch, the five books of Moses, as the opening books of the Bible are often known. We shall find that these stories that Matthew wants us to have in mind as we read about Jesus' temptations have a lot to say about you and me, not only about Israel of old.

Perhaps no event in the scriptural narrative of God's interaction with his chosen people is more central to Israel's religious imagination than the exodus from Egypt, the story in which the crossing of the wilderness of dust plays such a crucial role. But when we look back to the narrative of Israel's wanderings in the desert in the book of Exodus, we do not find it an account of a period of pure devotion to God on Israel's part. It would be more accurate to say that the wilderness period is a story of Israel's infidelity and rebellion against God. The key theme of the wilderness episodes in the book of Exodus, and in the various subsequent scriptural retellings of the story, is the constant testing of the covenant relationship established by God with Israel, a testing – or a series of temptations, we might say – that Israel systematically fails.

In each of the instances of the motif of dust that we are considering, both the clay from which humanity is shaped and the wilderness land through which the chosen community is led by God, the central image itself is initially unpromising; it is the divine initiative and activity, the breath or wind that carries God's Spirit, that works with the dead dust to produce the very stuff of life: the individual human person, *adam*, and also the human community, Israel. In

both cases, though, we know only too well in our own lives
that the dust can prove recalcitrant, crumbling in the hand
of the creator.

The story told in the book of Exodus of Israel's wilderness
journey only too clearly demonstrates the damage that
sin has worked in God's good creation, and in doing so it
uncovers the extent of the need for a new beginning. In
the Gospel story of Jesus' temptations, the New Testament
narrative dramatizes the redeeming activity of the saviour
of Israel to bring about just such a new beginning. We
watch as the divine craftsman breaks down and reshapes
the slippery clay of his human creation, unwilling that his
efforts should come to nothing. The parable of the potter
in the book of Jeremiah helps us to see the relationship
between Israel in the wilderness and the work of Jesus in
the desert:

> I went down to the potter's house, and there he was
> working at his wheel. The vessel he was making of clay
> was spoiled in the potter's hand, and he reworked it into
> another vessel, as seemed good to him. Then the word of
> the LORD came to me: Can I not do with you, O house
> of Israel, just as this potter has done? says the LORD. Just
> like the clay in the potter's hand, so are you in my hand, O
> house of Israel. (Jer. 18.3-6)

The New Testament story of the temptations is in direct
continuity with the story of Israel in the desert, just as the
clay remains one and the same material in Jeremiah's parable.
But God's new activity in Jesus represents a fulfilment of

Jeremiah's vision of this one clay reworked, made into another vessel 'as seemed good to him'.

When the psalmist looks back on Israel's wilderness years in his long historical poems, Psalms 78 and 106, the picture is one of Israel's constant striving against God:

> How often they rebelled against him in the wilderness
> and grieved him in the desert!
> They tested God again and again,
> and provoked the Holy One of Israel.
>
> (Ps. 78.40-41)

In this psalm we follow a story of divine acts of salvation systematically rejected by their recipients. This is what makes Psalm 78 such an ordeal for any of us to pray: the psalmist never allows us to lose sight of the sad history of sinful rebellion that has been the response of humanity, including ourselves, to divine generosity. As we pray this psalm, we follow Israel's journey of infidelity, and come to recognize the landscape as one we ourselves have trodden.

In another history psalm, Psalm 106, Israel's faithlessness begins as early as her time in Egypt, when Israel 'did not remember the abundance of your steadfast love' (Ps. 106.7). Two key Old Testament terms are deployed here: the active and engaged personal 'remembering' that implicates me in a relationship to that which I remember, and the term 'steadfast love', a word freighted with all the zeal and unceasing attention that the craftsman bestows on his masterpiece, as well as the warmth and concern that we find in the mother's protective love for her child. Sometimes translated as 'mercy' or 'loving kindness', even as 'grace', the Hebrew term has an energy that doesn't quite seem to surface in any of the English equivalents.

Throughout Psalm 106, Israel is depicted as 'forgetting' its relationship with God during the desert period. Idolatry is a particularly vicious manifestation of this sinfully amnesiac heart-set for the psalmist, a perversion of God's created order that leads Israel into the hellish practice of child sacrifice (vv. 37-38). When the dust of humanity falls away from the creator's hand, it seems only the howling wilderness waste remains, with all its potential to devour and to destroy. Both the psalms and the Old Testament prose tradition in the book of Exodus are unstinting in their critique of the failure of Israel to respond appropriately to the regularly manifested steadfast love of the redeeming God. If we are able to read and pray through this psalmic account of Israel's history of false choices, which we realize is also our own, we are facing the Lenten fact that, in Jeremiah's terms, the clay pot is spoiled. We are beginning to pray, with biblical Israel, for a new start to our relationship with God.

Alongside these frank biblical acknowledgements of the extent of Israel's desert infidelities, the Old Testament is also informed with a longing on the part of God's people to witness some kind of return to the desert period, a sort of 'second honeymoon', in order that the infidelity that so betrayed the saving work of God in the desert the first time might be put right. But there is a clear insistence in the prophetic books – where this imagery of a return to the desert is particularly to be found – that any 'new exodus', any second chance in the wilderness for a sinful nation, will be the work of God alone and not the consequence of any human initiative.

In chapter 2 of the book of Hosea, a prophetic work from the eighth century BCE, we discover a series of oracles that promise Israel a second chance, a return to the desert lands of her youth as a nation. In place of the infidelity and idolatry Israel has continued to practise, now in the fertile land of Canaan rather than in the wilderness, God will call her back to the desert. Here, God will offer his unfaithful spouse, Israel, a second opportunity to undergo the wilderness experience – and this time to remain in a right relationship with her God. The renewed desert journey is portrayed as a period of a purer relationship with the Lord:

> Therefore, I will now persuade her,
> and bring her into the wilderness,
> and speak tenderly to her.
> ...
> There she shall respond as in the days of her youth,
> as at the time when she came out of the land of Egypt.
>
> (Hos. 2.14-15)

Speaking in God's name, the prophet promises a new covenant between God and his people, a relationship reborn, close as that of husband and wife (see Hos. 2.16-23). This will be God's work, the prophet teaches, not in any sense the result of human initiatives. The later prophetic writings, especially the later chapters of the book of Isaiah, resound with the divine call to prepare for this new desert journey: 'In the wilderness prepare the way of the LORD, make straight in the desert a highway for our God' (Isa. 40.3). The desert journey is to take place again, and this time it will take place not in idolatry and rebellion but in righteousness and in justice, in steadfast love, and in mercy (see Hos. 2.16-20).

When we situate the story of Jesus' temptations in the desert (Mt. 4.1-11) against this Old Testament backcloth, we begin to see that in this story Matthew's Gospel is painting a picture of Jesus as himself the one in whom the prophetic promise of a return for Israel to the wilderness in a journey of trust and fidelity to God is to take place. In Matthew's narrative, Jesus himself is the 'New Israel' and it is by his activity that the desert period for the renewal of humanity's relationship with our creator can finally come about – precisely through the divine initiative, as had been prophesied. Our place in this story becomes more apparent: we are those on whose behalf Jesus, in the wilderness, is opening up the possibility of a new relationship with God founded upon fidelity.

Matthew has a habit of quoting texts of Old Testament scripture that he tells us are 'being fulfilled' in Jesus. For example, immediately after Jesus' birth in Bethlehem, Matthew tells of the slaughter of the new-born children carried out by King Herod, and the subsequent flight of Joseph and Mary with the child Jesus to the safety of Egypt until Herod was dead. This, the Gospel writer tells us, 'was to fulfil what had been spoken by the Lord through the prophet, "Out of Egypt I have called my son"' (Mt. 2.15) – for Matthew, this is the beginning of the new exodus.

Matthew's narrative is constructed around a theology of the fulfilment of God's promises by Jesus, and this use of the Old Testament in short quotations is one of the ways in which Matthew informs us that whatever happens in the life and ministry of Jesus has already been foretold by God. Jesus' activity is shown to be a manifestation of the steadfast love and faithfulness of Israel's God, the one who keeps his promises. These texts are used by Matthew to make the same point we find in Saint Luke's Gospel, where Jesus says 'everything written about me in the law of Moses, the prophets, and the psalms must be fulfilled' (Lk. 24.44). For Matthew, Jesus is himself the new exodus, the new beginning, and the new beginning is a faithful fulfilment of what has gone before.

The crucial challenge failed by Israel, 'a stubborn and rebellious generation' (Ps. 78.8), in the exodus desert journey was the challenge of remaining steadfast in obedience to God. Obedience was tested for Israel, and obedience failed, in the threefold challenge of food, adherence to God's promises and worshipping other gods. Where Israel failed, the new beginning God provides lies in the obedience of Jesus to his mission, his standing against the devil's temptations in all their forms by placing his faith directly and solely in the God of Israel. In Jesus' repeated refrain 'it is written' (Mt. 4.4, 7, 10) there is expressed an attachment to the promises of Israel's God that was sorely lacking on the part of the exodus generation. What we see in Jesus' desert journey is a Gospel portrait of the one who, as the letter to the Hebrews puts it, 'Although he was a Son ... learned obedience through what he suffered; and having been made perfect, he became the source of eternal salvation for all who obey him' (Heb. 5.8-9).

Matthew's story of the temptations offers us an account of the divine craftsman still at his labours. The clay of Israel's sin is reshaped to become the raw material of a new Israel, to become indeed 'a chosen race, a royal priesthood, a holy nation, God's own people, in order that you may proclaim the mighty acts of him who called you out of darkness into his marvellous light' (1 Pet. 2.9). 'Can I not do with you, O house of Israel, just as this potter has done?' Jeremiah heard God ask. In the temptations narrative we witness God's fulfilment, in the person of Jesus, of the prophetic promise of the new exodus, the journey of obedience through the desert. Far more, in fact, than a simple reshaping of a spoiled pot into a better vessel, this event is the beginning of a renewal of the whole created order, a restoration and perfection of the relationship between God and his human creation.

Such an understanding of the temptations narrative emerges clearly at the very end of this Gospel story, where a restoration of the relationship of humanity with God that existed in the garden of paradise is pictured, as the devil flees from Christ 'and suddenly angels came and waited on him' (Mt. 4.11). Jesus is shown to us here as the perfected human creature Adam was to be but never became. Where our first parents were driven from the garden by the angel sent by God to expel humanity from paradise, Jesus – the new Adam – is served by angels in a wilderness that now, by his obedience, becomes the garden of a creation being refashioned and made new. Our exploration of dust, which began in the soil of the garden of Eden, finds us returning to a restored paradise as Jesus re-establishes the order of God's good creation by his trusting solely in God as he works once again in the wilderness of dry dust.

2

The Mountain: The Second Week of Lent

Six days later, Jesus took with him Peter and James and his brother John and led them up a high mountain, by themselves. (Mt. 17.1)

You don't need to travel extensively across the landscape of the psalms to encounter hills and mountains. Like the land of Israel, the territory of the psalmist abounds in mountainous hill country, and the imagery deployed in these poems reflects this fact. Occasionally, psalmic hills are found to be outrageously vital, leaping like rams or yearling sheep in Psalm 114, the skipping hills offering images that express the wonder of the creation at God's manifestation in history as saviour. More usually, as in Psalm 125, the towering mountains cannot be shaken and stand for ever; they serve to express the fidelity of the covenant God in whom Israel trusts, 'As the mountains surround Jerusalem, so the LORD surrounds his people, from this time on and for evermore' (Ps. 125.2). Sometimes shrouded by cloud, and at other times the sites of fiery light-storms, the mountains of Israel feature regularly in the imaginative environment of the psalmist.

But, as Psalm 48 demonstrates, the psalms also know of a specific 'holy mountain of God', a single place associated with the relationship between God and his people. This is Mount Zion, where God's Temple is situated in Jerusalem:

> His holy mountain, beautiful in elevation,
> is the joy of all the earth,
> Mount Zion, in the far north,
> the city of the great king.
>
> (Ps. 48.1-2)

This mountain is clearly located in Israel's historical and geographical experience of God's saving action. But when the holy mountain is celebrated in the psalms, its attributes begin to sound rather more than simply geographical. For Psalm 78, Mount Zion can be likened to the very heavens; it stands firm as the ground on which we stand: 'He built his sanctuary like the high heavens, like the earth, which he has founded for ever' (Ps. 78.69). Zion, beautiful in elevation in the far north, or likened to the cosmos God has 'founded for ever', is not being pictured as a simple Judean hill.

In fact, as any visitor to the Dome of the Rock, the site of the now-vanished Temple in present-day Jerusalem, can see, the Temple 'mountain' is one among several relatively unimposing hills in and around Jerusalem, and not a particularly high one at that. It also isn't in the north of Israel, where Psalm 48 places it. 'There is a river whose streams make glad the city of God, the holy habitation of the Most High' (Ps. 46.4), sings the psalmist. Only, there isn't a river on Mount Zion, as Jerusalem's rulers knew only too well to their and their people's cost in times of warfare and siege, when water supply became a critical issue. The imagery of this holy mountain is not really derived from its geography at all, but from symbolic motifs deployed by the psalmist to speak of the closeness of the relationship between God and his chosen people.

From looking towards the dust beneath our feet, the Gospel of the second Sunday of Lent, the transfiguration (Mt. 17.1-13), prompts us to raise our gaze from the depths and points us towards the high places of the earth, as Jesus takes three of his closest disciples up a high mountain. Just as is the case with the holy mountain of the psalms, we shall discover that the mountain of the transfiguration is used by the writer of the Gospel as a symbol that can help us understand something of God's activity both in the scriptural texts and in our lives.

Christian tradition identifies the mountain of Jesus' transfiguration as Mount Tabor, an abrupt and almost unnaturally conical hill that erupts from the surrounding Galilean plains of the Jezreel valley, to the west of the Sea of Galilee. I have dizzying memories of braving the vertiginous ascent to the peak of Tabor some years ago, on my one and only visit to the Holy Land. But attractive as it is to identify geographical locales that allow us to follow in the literal footsteps of Jesus and his disciples, the story Matthew's Gospel tells in chapter 17 is less concerned with the physical geography of Palestine than it is with the sacred geography of Jesus' mission as Messiah: Matthew wants us to focus on the meaning of the event and on what its mountain-top setting tells us about our salvation in Christ.

In the previous chapter, the writing in the dust led us to
a story set in the garden of Eden, where we explored the
significance of God's shaping of humanity from the ground
of the earth, as told in Genesis chapter 2. To begin our
exploration of scripture's understanding of the heights of
the earth and our ascent of the mountain of transfiguration,
we begin by once again visiting the garden of God, this
time in the company of a different storyteller, the prophet
Ezekiel.

THE HOLY MOUNTAIN OF GOD

Ezekiel is a prophet called by God to work in the dark years
of the sixth century BCE, a period when God's people were
carried into exile by the world power of the time, Babylon.
His lengthy prophetic book abounds in astonishing images,
visions and parables through which he strives to understand
and to express, on behalf of a struggling, fractured nation,
how the dark history of his age continues to be shaped by the
guiding hand of a faithful God. One strategy Ezekiel uses to
achieve this end is to bring into Israel's present awareness
aspects of its past sacred tradition that have slipped away from
immediate focus, in order to grasp insights from the past that
may throw light on God's present-day dealings both with his
chosen people and with the nations among whom Israel has
been scattered.

We noticed in the previous chapter that the book of
Genesis knows of two similar but not identical accounts of
God's activity in creating humanity. Ezekiel, in drawing upon
Israel's memory to speak of God's activity in his own time, at

one point makes use of a third set of ideas about God's work in the forming of humanity. The passage in Ezekiel 28.11-19 is one of great rhetorical solemnity, appearing as part of a series of oracles that declare the fall of the neighbouring coastal nation of Tyre, said to have become proud and corrupt through its trading wealth. The story of the creation of humanity in the garden of Eden is used by Ezekiel to contrast the perfection and giftedness of Tyre's beginnings with its present decadence and fall from grace. But the differences between this version of the Eden story in Ezekiel and that of Genesis 2 are very striking.

In Ezekiel 28, Eden remains the garden we know from Genesis, but it is pictured not on a wide plain but as located rather upon what the prophet calls 'the holy mountain of God' (Ezek. 28.14,16), a seemingly volcanic height described as shining with stones of fire and supervised by an 'anointed guardian cherub' placed by God to watch over the perfect human creature God has made. In Ezekiel's telling, the first human being is endowed with royal, almost divine, dignity and clothed magnificently in gold and precious gemstones, 'carnelian, chrysolite, and moonstone, beryl, onyx, and jasper, sapphire, turquoise, and emerald' (v. 13); not only glorious to see, but able to walk safely among the stones of fire, just as the cherubs do. We are told that God makes humanity perfect in wisdom, and blameless in their ways, and that this bright, fiery beauty belonged to humanity 'until iniquity was found in you' (v. 15). Like the Genesis story, Ezekiel's creation narrative includes a fall from wisdom and integrity for humanity: 'so I cast you as a profane thing from the mountain of God, and the guardian cherub drove you out from among the stones of fire' (v. 16).

At first glance, Ezekiel's image of the mountain of Eden and its glorious inhabitant can give the reader quite a jolt – it seems at such variance with the story told in Genesis 2, where a simple tiller of the soil lives naked among the trees of the first garden. The glowing, bejewelled demi-god of Ezekiel 28 has been significantly 'transfigured', we might say. But it's worth reminding ourselves of how the significance of God's creation of the human race, and thus humanity's original dignity before the fall, is emphasized by both the Genesis creation stories, in their very different idioms: in chapter 1, by the placing of humanity's creation at the climax of the six days of God's ordering of the cosmos, in God's image and likeness, with dominion over the whole natural world; in chapter 2, by the intimate, direct congress of God with his human creation, shaped by his hands, animated by his breath, guided personally by his instructions. The psalmist recognizes the same created dignity: humanity is created 'a little lower than God', says Psalm 8, crowned with honour and glory and given dominion over all God's handiwork (Ps. 8.5-8). Thus the 'transfigured' humanity on the holy mountain of God in Ezekiel 28 serves as a sign of all that God originally intended for his human creation, and acts as an anticipation of the renewed humanity of the kingdom of God. Ezekiel's retelling of the Eden story invites us to notice the biblical connection between the holy mountain where God is made known among his people, and humanity fully alive as God purposed.

We know from study of the sacred texts of ancient Israel's historic neighbours that many Near-Eastern cultures of the millennia before Christ located the domain of the divine, and the first place created in the world, on a mountain-top, the 'holy mountain of God'. In the mythologies of Mesopotamia, where the exiled Ezekiel lived among his defeated and deported compatriots, a holy mountain was regarded as the site of divine creativity and the locus of worship in the god's temple: the mountain-temple of the creator-god being held to represent the first aspect of the created order to emerge from the chaos ocean, and forming an 'omphalos', a centre or navel to the world, as it was then understood by the peoples of the land of the two rivers.

When we set it against this background, the retelling of the Eden story in Ezekiel 28 throws light on some of the otherwise puzzling imagery deployed by the psalmist in speaking of Mount Zion. So, for example, the 'river whose streams make glad the city of God' in Psalm 46 is not a river that can be archeologically unearthed, concealed beneath the sand and stones of the historic Temple mount. But a river does flow from the holy mountain of God in the creation tradition Ezekiel is referencing in chapter 28. It is the same river that the Eden story in the book of Genesis tells us about: 'a river flows out of Eden to water the garden' (Gen. 2.10). This river flows from the holy mountain, or in some other biblical traditions from the Temple of God built on the mountain. Such images of the river on the Temple mountain feature in visions of future salvation in the Old Testament prophet Zechariah, who speaks of 'living waters' that shall flow out from Jerusalem (Zech. 14.8), while Ezekiel's own vision of a restored and glorified Temple in the later chapters of his book includes an extended treatment of a mighty torrent flowing from beneath the Temple, and watering the surrounding landscape (Ezek. 47.1-12). The book of Revelation, at the end of the New Testament, has in mind these and other scriptural moments when its visionary author builds on the imagery of Psalm 46 to describe 'the river of the water of life, bright as crystal, flowing from the throne of God and of the Lamb through the middle of the street of the city' (Rev. 22.1-2).

Biblical Israel, then, has its own traditions of a 'holy mountain of God', and uses motifs such as the life-giving river or the exalted height of the mountain to associate Zion with God's original act of the creation of the world, as well as utilizing the same motifs to speak of God's salvific remaking of his creation in the end days. Recognizing this version of the mountain theme running through the presentation of Jerusalem and the Temple helps us see what is happening when the psalmist prays for God's intervention from his holy mountain (see Ps. 3.4) or speaks of climbing the mountain of the Lord (see Ps. 24.3). It also enriches our appreciation of the compelling vision of future peace announced by the prophets Isaiah and Micah:

In days to come
the mountain of the LORD's house
shall be established as the highest of the mountains,
and shall be raised above the hills;
all the nations shall stream to it.

(Isa. 2.2, cf. Mic. 4.1-5)

In Israel's prophetic tradition, the hope for future peace and prosperity across all the earth finds expression in a renewed and glorified presence of God on his holy mountain at the centre of the world. In Isaiah's vision, Zion is physically endowed with the grandeur it has metaphorically enjoyed throughout the psalmic tradition and elsewhere; the rivers of flowing water pouring from the mountain are reimagined as an inflowing of the peoples of the whole earth towards the Temple of the God of Israel:

> Many peoples shall come and say,
> 'Come, let us go up to the mountain of the LORD,
> to the house of the God of Jacob;
> that he may teach us his ways
> and that we may walk in his paths.'
>
> (Isa. 2.3)

When we place this vision in the context of the creation story that features a holy mountain and the mountain imagery we see in the psalms, we are better able to grasp the ways in which Isaiah's prophecy foretells the healing of the divisions between peoples described in the Babel story in the book of Genesis, the re-admission of exiled humanity to the garden of God from which it has been banished, and above all the reintegration of God's human creation with its creator in obedience to his ways and the following of his paths: 'For out of Zion shall go forth instruction, and the word of the LORD from Jerusalem' (Isa. 2.3). As we ponder Isaiah's richly imagined oracle, we begin to recognize that the prophet is in fact speaking of a redemptive rolling-back of the entire history of sin and separation from God consequent upon the fall of humanity, and the re-establishment of the Edenic order of the creation, as intended by its creator. For the psalmist, as for the prophetic tradition, it is this salvific work that sits as the central significance of the motif of the 'holy mountain of God'.

There is a form of poetic engagement with the language and imagery of salvation at work in these texts that lends itself to our prayerful reflection. Sometimes, to pray with scripture is to step into a colourful and densely realized landscape – not in order to have any specific outcome in terms of articulated ideas, but more to marvel at the beauty of what is depicted in the scriptural account of God's saving work. To climb Ezekiel's holy mountain and stand with our first parent among the stones of fire, or to make pilgrimage with Isaiah to the Temple on Mount Zion as whole nations stream in longing towards it, may feel initially strange. Especially if we have become accustomed solely to forms of prayer that discourage the making of mental pictures. But the special effects departments of movie studios would have to work overtime to populate our imaginations with better pictures than these, and even then would fall far short of offering a script that matches the one that God has assembled to accompany these pictures. Salvation in Christ does not exist in the abstract – our concrete lives are its locus. And it is from the pictures we form in our minds, the scripts we learn and then carry into our everyday encounters, that our best selves can be moulded by the word of God. God's pictures make powerful precepts.

THE MOUNTAIN OF ZION WHICH HE LOVES

The Old Testament narrative associates the God of Abraham, Isaac and Jacob very especially with two different mountains in the course of Israel's history. The lengthy account of sacred history in Psalm 78 celebrates each of them. The first is Mount Sinai (which, rather confusingly, is also called Horeb in some Old Testament traditions), to which God leads Israel through the wilderness after the crossing of the Red Sea:

> He led them in safety, so that they were not afraid;
> but the sea overwhelmed their enemies.
> And he brought them to his holy hill,
> to the mountain that his right hand had won.

> (Ps. 78.53-54)

In the narrative of the book of Exodus, it is at Sinai that the law of life, the *torah*, is given to Moses, and the covenant between God and Israel is established. As Psalm 78 suggests, Israel's arrival at Sinai is the culminating moment in the story of the exodus from Egypt. The Exodus narrative makes plain that the 'mountain of God' is a holy place of revelation, a site where God manifests himself in all his glory – the imagery of Sinai is one of fire, smoke and storm; thunder and lightning and the blasts of a great trumpet accompany the presence of God on the mountain (see Exod. 19). Early in the story of Moses, it is on Sinai that the future leader of God's people first encounters the God of Abraham, in the theophany of the burning bush (Exod. 3.1-21), and it is to this same mountain that he is commanded to return with the Israelites after their deliverance from Egypt. The divine injunction issued to Moses from the fiery bush, 'Come no closer! Remove the sandals from your feet, for the place on which you are standing is holy ground' (Exod. 3.5), represents the Sinai tradition of the mountain's holiness, and also makes clear the physical danger that this holiness poses to mere mortals.

Old Testament Israel conceptualized God's transcendent otherness as a radical separateness from the human realm – God is wholly what mortal creatures are not, and therefore wholly separate from us, as we are from God. If the mortal creature strays into the realm of the wholly other, the Exodus tradition teaches, something akin to what modern imaginations might picture as the collision of matter with anti-matter will take place: 'the LORD will break out against them' (Exod. 19.22). A recurrent theme of those Old Testament texts that have to do with the practicalities of public worship is the detail of the preparations, both ritual and moral, necessary for safely coming close to the God of Israel.

There is a genuinely awful majesty to the Sinai understanding of God's presence. We see it in Isaiah's temple vision, in the course of which the prophet cries out in terror at the sight of God's glorious presence (see Isa. 6.1-7). But for those other than Moses, with whom God speaks face to face, as with a friend (see Exod. 33.11), the foot of the mountain was the closest to God that they were permitted to come. At Sinai, God's revelation could only be manifest to them as fire, smoke and blasts of sound. While scripture is always permeated with awareness of God's transcendent holiness, the unfolding of biblical revelation through the books of the Old Testament and into the New can be read at one level as the story of how Israel comes to understand more fully the answer to the psalmist's question: 'Who shall ascend the hill of the LORD? And who shall stand in his holy place' (Ps. 24.3), and is inspired to understand that there is no narrowness to the love of God, but rather breadth and length and height and depth.

An important part of the way this broader answer comes about is to be discovered in the form of the second 'holy mountain' identified in Psalm 78, Mount Zion, the hill of the Temple in Jerusalem:

... he chose the tribe of Judah,
Mount Zion, which he loves.
He built his sanctuary like the high heavens,
like the earth, which he has founded for ever

(Ps. 78.68-69)

The first holy mountain, Sinai, plays a crucial role in Israel's journey to becoming the people of God in the land promised to them, but it is ultimately superseded in biblical thought by the hill of Zion in Jerusalem. As Mount Zion, the location of Solomon's Temple, this relatively modest hill becomes the 'holy mountain of God' *par excellence* for the psalmist and for the later texts of the Old Testament.

The two holy mountains have features in common, but there are also significant differences between them. While motifs of divine presence, of the law of God, and an imagery of fire and cloud are associated with both locations, Sinai is always characterized in the imagery of separation as a forbidding and dangerous place, inaccessible to all but the few, whereas 'Zion, which he loves' (Ps. 78.68) regularly evokes an imagery of longing and desire, especially as it is presented in the psalms: 'I was glad when they said to me, "Let us go to the house of the LORD!"' (Ps. 122.1). Unlike Sinai, Zion is pictured as the universal home to which all members of the house of Israel are to be gathered, in order to enjoy God's blessings. In the psalms, God will even gather the least of Israel to his mountain: 'The LORD ... gathers the outcasts of Israel' (Ps. 147.2-3). And we have seen how the prophetic oracles will speak of an ultimate ingathering not only of Israel but also of the whole earth to the Temple mountain of God.

Whereas Sinai represents God's awesome holiness as separation from all but a few of his people, the Temple on Mount Zion is the place where Israel's God has graciously chosen to make himself available to the prayer of all his people. The holy mountain of Zion is the Old Testament's most potent symbol of God's closeness to his human creation. For the psalmist, it is the physical site of the Temple on its hill in Jerusalem that stands as a visible sign that 'the LORD of hosts is with us; the God of Jacob is our refuge' (Ps. 46.7, 11). The blessing of God's presence and power on Mount Zion is understood as securing the wellbeing of his people, and especially of the mountain where the Temple itself stands: 'God is in the midst of the city; it shall not be moved; God will help it when the morning dawns' (Ps. 46.5).

When the prophet Isaiah offers a sign from God to King Ahaz in a situation where Jerusalem is threatened by war, it is this: 'Look, the young woman is with child and shall bear a son, and shall name him Immanuel' (Isa. 7.14). At the heart of the oracle is the name 'Immanuel', a name that means 'God is with us'. Isaiah invites the king, and thus the whole nation, to place their trust in the God who makes himself accessible on Mount Zion, 'God with us' – this is the only sign God's people need of their God's desire to be present as saviour. For the psalmist the same is true: 'Be still, and know that I am God!' (Ps. 46.10) is an expression of trust in the God who dwells on Zion and 'makes wars cease to the end of the earth' (Ps. 46.9).

Although Zion is the place where God invites the least and the greatest of his people to stand before him, the psalms nonetheless make plain that human beings do not and cannot approach God in a merely casual manner, without a moral seriousness. We find this point emphatically stressed in the psalms that were written to accompany those who entered the precincts of God's holy hill. Psalm 24, for example, suggests what has sometimes been called an 'entrance liturgy' for the Temple in Jerusalem. It is constructed as a dialogue between different voices that may have formed part of a public act of worship at the Temple gates, perhaps a procession of some kind. The psalm begins, like many prayers having to do with the Temple, by evoking the creator God, who has established the cosmic order: 'The earth is the LORD's and all that is in it, the world, and those who live in it' (Ps. 24.1). It is with this awareness of the awesome creator of the macrocosm of the cosmos, who deigns to be present in one specific location, the microcosm of the Temple, that the psalm then asks: 'Who shall ascend the hill of the LORD? And who shall stand in his holy place?' (Ps. 24.3). Such a question could not have been asked at Mount Sinai.

Psalm 15, another song that seems to involve a liturgical procession into the Temple, which it understands as God's earthy abode or tent, begins with a similar direct challenge: 'O LORD, who may abide in your tent? Who may dwell on your holy hill?' (Ps. 15.1). Both psalms go on to present a list of the moral qualities of those who shall 'ascend the hill of the LORD'. It is as if both psalms constitute a formal examination of conscience before approaching the presence of the Lord. In Psalm 24 it is 'Those who have clean hands and pure hearts' (Ps. 24.4) who will receive the blessing of admission to the presence of the God of Jacob. Psalm 15 speaks of those 'who walk blamelessly, and do what is right, and speak the truth from their heart' (Ps. 15.2). The blessing of God's presence on his holy hill belongs to those of whom the Gospel says: 'Blessed are the pure in heart, for they will see God' (Mt. 5.8).

Because of the use of the expression 'songs of Zion' in Psalm 137.3, where it is the designation of the temple prayers that exiled Israel's captors call for in mockery, a small group of psalms scattered throughout the psalter whose focus is specifically the Temple mountain have become known as 'Zion songs'. Psalm 84, a lyrical evocation of devotion to the holy hill, begins, 'How lovely is your dwelling place, O LORD of hosts!' (Ps. 84.1). God's gift of his presence at the heart of Israel's worship never fails to generate celebration in these Zion psalms. The psalmist exclaims: 'Happy are those whose strength is in you, in whose heart are the highways to Zion'

(Ps. 84.5). In the light of the entrance liturgies such as Psalms 15 and 24, we can see that the image of the 'highways to Zion' in the heart of the believer is a metaphor supporting the tradition of moral integrity and uprightness: it is the heart that is pure and lives in truth that holds the highway whereby we travel to see the face of God.

As Psalm 84 unfolds we discover a number of images that once again connect the Jerusalem Temple with God's beneficent creation of the cosmos. The Lord God is associated by the psalmist with the very light of the sun and the cool shade in the heat (v. 11), his altars form a shelter for the birds of the air (v. 3), who build nests and raise their young within the Temple, and in verses 5-7 the pilgrims who travel the highways to Zion prove a life-bestowing blessing for the wilderness territory they pass through, as 'they make it a place of springs; the early rain also covers it with pools'. The creation is evoked in the mention of living creatures, the light and the fructifying waters. Accounts of the Temple and its contents such as that of 1 Kings 7, make plain that Solomon's Temple was designed to stand as a microcosm of the whole of God's created order. The Temple on the holy mountain always represented the eternal presence of the creator God within the natural sanctuary of his entire world as detailed in the creation narratives.

But the central claim of all the Zion songs is the astonishing truth of God's presence and accessibility; each psalm in its own way articulates the close association of the presence of God with the Temple on the holy mountain. Each of these songs of Zion renews the boast of Psalm 46: 'God is in the midst of the city; it shall not be moved; God will help it when the morning dawns' (Ps. 46.5). The most vividly imagined form of the claim is to be found in Psalm 48, which invites its hearer to 'walk about Zion ... count its towers ... that you may tell the next generation that this is God, our God for ever and ever' (Ps. 48.12-14). In this psalm, the physical presence of the Temple on Mount Zion becomes a concrete local metaphor, a geographical correlate standing for the accessibility and closeness of the God of Israel in the midst of his people. One might almost say that the psalmist looks towards an 'incarnation' of the presence of Israel's God among his people.

THE MOUNTAIN OF TRANSFIGURATION

Like the psalmist, the author of Matthew's Gospel displays a particular fascination with mountains. The first in canonical order of the Gospels presents us with a particularly densely patterned narrative structure, weaving together a series of recurring motifs that bear much of the symbolic ballast of the book. Taken together, they point us towards this Gospel's most important insights into the meaning of Jesus and his mission on earth. The motif of the mountain that figures in the story of the transfiguration has its roots firmly planted in the tradition of the 'holy mountain of God' and finds a clear place within one of Matthew's meaning-making patterns.

Perhaps the best known of the structures Matthew sets up in his narrative is what is often called the five-discourse pattern. As we saw in chapter 1, Matthew's Gospel presents

Jesus as the completion of everything that God began to work among his people through the leadership of Moses. To help underline this point, Matthew structures his account of Jesus' preaching and teaching into five continuous sections of teaching or 'discourses', placed at intervals throughout his Gospel. It seems that he has done this in order deliberately to mirror the five books of Moses (Genesis, Exodus, Numbers, Leviticus and Deuteronomy), the *torah* or law of the Old Covenant, which Matthew wishes us to understand as fulfilled in the New Covenant brought by the new Moses, Jesus.

The mountain motif in Matthew's Gospel does not have the same major structuring role in his narrative as the five-discourse pattern; nevertheless, Matthew's choice to locate on mountains five moments in Jesus' ministry, as well as the final appearance of the risen Jesus to commission his church, makes plain that the Gospel writer is associating this series of six events together in a particular way. We have already met one of the mountains of Matthew in his account of the temptations of Jesus (Mt. 4.8), and the Sermon on the Mount in Matthew 5 is the second. In Matthew 15.29-39 Jesus climbs a third mountain, where he will feed the four thousand who follow him there. When we reach the story of the transfiguration, we again go up a mountain (Mt. 17.1-9), as Jesus does a fifth and final time during his teaching ministry in Mt. 24.3 when, climbing to the Mount of Olives, he speaks to his disciples about the last days. It is in Mt. 28.16 that we reach the principal resurrection story in Matthew's Gospel, as the 11 disciples arrive in Galilee, at 'the mountain to which Jesus had directed them' (Mt. 28.16). It is here on the mountain that Jesus commissions them, as his church, to go out to call other disciples and to baptize in his name.

The Gospel of Matthew tells the story of Jesus from within a community of Christians who have an unusually deep knowledge of the Old Testament scriptures, to which this Gospel's author makes frequent reference, both direct and indirect. One particular manifestation of Matthew's deep dive into the beliefs and traditions of Israel as they help uncover the truth about Jesus can help us understand why Matthew locates the six events we have just identified on mountain-tops.

Matthew both begins and ends his account of 'Jesus the Messiah, the son of David, the son of Abraham' (Mt. 1.1) by explicitly associating Jesus with elements of Old Testament thought that find the divine presence among God's people on the holy mountain, the tradition of Mount Zion. As we have seen, this can be summed up in the psalmic exclamation, 'the LORD of hosts is with us' (Ps. 46.7). As Matthew offers his account of how the birth of Jesus came about, he reaches to that text of Isaiah in which the name 'Immanuel' figures. This Isaianic passage is associated with the tradition of God's saving presence on Mount Zion (see Isa. 7.14). For Matthew's Gospel: 'All this took place to fulfil what had been spoken by the Lord through the prophet: "Look, the virgin shall conceive and bear a son, and they shall name him Emmanuel", which means, "God is with us"' (Mt. 1.22-23).

Matthew associates the angelic injunction to Joseph that Mary's son is to be called 'Jesus', 'for he will save his people from their sins' (Mt. 1.21), with the name 'Emmanuel' – the symbolic name for the salvific presence of God on the holy mountain. Jesus is identified by Matthew's Gospel, even before he is born, as the one in whom the saving presence of God on the holy mountain is now at work in a wholly personal manner.

By way of an *inclusio*, a use of that literary technique we have met before whereby an author 'wraps around' his key point so that it frames the material upon which it casts light, Matthew returns to the theme of 'God is with us' as he brings his Gospel to an end. On the mountain in Galilee where the risen Jesus greets his startled friends, it is Jesus' words 'I am with you always, to the end of the age' (Mt. 28.20) that bring this Gospel narrative to a close. So Matthew's account of the gospel of Jesus Christ is framed by the Mount Zion message of divine presence as saviour in the midst of Israel, 'the LORD of hosts is with us', now manifested personally in the Son of God, Jesus the Messiah. Matthew's message about Jesus is informed from beginning to end by an awareness of the theology of the holy mountain of God, the earthly locus of God's presence, now manifested in a new and marvellous way.

Between the two framing brackets of the *inclusio*, Matthew shapes his Gospel to include the six mountain-top moments that were referenced earlier. We might imagine an early Christian reader who has lived for many years within Israel's tradition of the holy mountain of God, who ponders Matthew's telling of such a story. This reader would perhaps find the mountain, the biblical place where God makes himself present among his people and manifests his life-giving *torah* to Israel, a very appropriate place for the Son of

God to stand when he opens up a new space of obedience to God for a renewed humanity on the mountain of temptation, or when – like a new Moses – he renews the *torah* of God, offering guidance from God for human life in the present in the Sermon on the Mount or for the future in the Olivet discourse.

Such a reader would not be surprised to find that, just as in the psalms where God's faithful 'feast on the abundance of your house, and you give them drink from the river of your delights' (Ps. 36.8) on the holy mountain of Zion, it was on another mountain that Jesus, the one in whom 'God is with us', ensured that the crowd following him were able to eat and to have their fill (see Mt. 15.36-37), departing like the psalmist leaving the mountain of the Temple 'satisfied as with a rich feast' (Ps. 63.5). We begin to see that the mountain range Matthew has built through the length of his Gospel exists to manifest, at these points within his narrative, the divine nature of the one who is 'God with us'.

Of the six mountain-top passages in his Gospel, one that Matthew especially wants us to notice is in Matthew 28.16-20, where we find the story of the resurrection of Jesus, and the commissioning of his disciples. This story makes explicit one of the ways in which the earlier mountain stories, including the transfiguration, are to be understood. In chapter 28, Jesus appears to his disciples on the mountain as the one upon whom all authority has been bestowed, as is the case in Psalm 2 where it is announced by God that 'I have set my king on Zion, my holy hill' (Ps. 2.6). Like the king of Psalm 2, Jesus has been identified twice in Matthew's narrative with words borrowed from this same psalm, 'You are my son; today I have begotten you' (Ps. 2.7) – at his baptism and in the account of the transfiguration in chapter 17. And again, like the king of Psalm 2, Jesus claims the allegiance of 'all nations', whom the disciples are commissioned to gather within their risen master's kingly rule: 'Ask of me, and I will make the nations your heritage, and the ends of the earth your possession' are God's words to the king in the psalm (Ps. 2.8).

Psalm 2 brings the tradition of the presence of God on the holy mountain together with the idea of a future ideal ruler, a universal king, who will inaugurate a kingdom of justice and truth among all the peoples of the world. In chapter 28, Matthew pictures the risen Jesus, who is the very presence of God among us, on the mountain and beginning to exercise this kingly rule over the peoples through the mission of his church, which is sent out to preach and baptize. This understanding of who Jesus really is has an importance as we approach Matthew's narrative of the transfiguration.

Matthew wants us to recognize that the mountain is the symbolic place where we are most fully able to understand who Jesus really is. In this Gospel, it is when we see him on a mountain that Jesus, in whom God is present among his people, clearly shows himself as the fulfilment of the traditions associated with the sacred mountain of the Old Testament. As such, he is to be understood throughout the Gospel narrative as he is revealed to be in the chapter 28 resurrection story as the one of whom Psalm 2 says: 'I have set my king on Zion, my holy hill' (Ps. 2.6). When Jesus is presented by Matthew on the mountain-top, the Gospel writer intends that we should have in mind each mountain as a local version of Zion itself, the place where God is especially present, where his nature as saviour of Israel is most clearly manifest. At the same time, the final mountain passage, in chapter 28, helps us see that Jesus is understood to be the saviour-king established by God in Psalm 2, to whom God has declared: 'You are my son; today I have begotten you' (Ps. 2.7).

We are told that the events of the transfiguration in Matthew 17.1-13 take place 'six days later' (v. 1); six days after the momentous statement by Peter at Caesarea Philippi in Matthew 16, in which Simon Peter confesses Jesus to be 'the Messiah, the Son of the living God'. Jesus responds to him, 'Blessed are you, Simon son of Jonah! For flesh and blood has not revealed this to you, but my Father in heaven' (Mt. 16.17).

Why do precisely six days pass between these two events, placing the transfiguration on the seventh day? As modern readers, we have become accustomed to expecting historical literalism from accounts of times and dates, as if they were entries in our own work diaries; the writer and earliest readers of this story expected and understood a different approach, hearing symbolic echoes of the Old Testament throughout the Gospel narrative of Jesus' ministry and passion. Here, for example, the 'six days' echo both the six days of creation in Genesis chapter 1 that precede God's Sabbath rest on the seventh day, and the account of the theophany, the appearance of God, to Moses on Mount Sinai: 'The glory of the LORD settled on Mount Sinai, and the cloud covered it for six days; on the seventh day he called to Moses out of the cloud' (Exod. 24.16). The transfiguration story is written for an audience that is familiar with this narrative in the book of Exodus, and so knows that on the seventh day God calls to Moses out of the cloud, and 'the appearance of the glory of the LORD was like a devouring fire on the top of the mountain in the sight of the people of Israel. Moses entered the cloud, and went up on the mountain' (Exod. 24.17-18).

One of Matthew's purposes in the transfiguration story is to present Jesus as the new Moses, the 'prophet like me' promised by Moses to the people of Israel (Deut. 18.15), and so the actions of Jesus and his three disciples have parallels to some of the events of Exodus 24, as Moses ascends the mountain of God accompanied by three companions (see Exod. 24.9). The shining garments and imagery of light can also be seen as echoes of the imagery of the Moses story, in which the patriarch's face shines as a consequence of his encounter with God. But Matthew's story, as we might expect, is making an even stronger claim about the person of Jesus, and it is the imagery of the 'glory of God' that we find also in the Exodus account that plays the central role in making his point.

In the story of the theophany to Moses in the book of Exodus the 'glory of the LORD' descends upon the mountain. Here in Matthew's Gospel, in the passage immediately preceding the transfiguration story, we have heard Jesus say that 'the Son of Man is to come with his angels in the glory of his Father' (Mt. 16.27). It is an anticipation of precisely this vision of the glory of God that is granted to the three disciples who accompany Jesus onto the mountain; what Saint Paul calls 'the light of the knowledge of the glory of God in the face of Jesus Christ' (2 Cor. 4.6). Here, the glory of God is manifested in and around Jesus with an imagery of bright cloud, light and transformation of appearance. The mountain of transfiguration is revealed as a greater mountain than Sinai, where Moses was told that he would see the glory of God pass by, but would not be granted sight of the Lord's face (see Exod. 33). On this New Testament mountain, Peter, James and John are privileged to be the first witnesses to the glory that Matthew records as present in the risen Christ in Matthew 28, and which is spoken of in the second letter of Saint Peter:

> For he received honour and glory from God the Father when that voice was conveyed to him by the Majestic Glory, saying, 'This is my Son, my Beloved, with whom I am well pleased.' We ourselves heard this voice come from heaven, while we were with him on the holy mountain. (2 Pet. 1.16-18)

Most especially, the 'bright cloud' that overshadows the mountain of transfiguration represents the glory of the Lord, recalling the cloud of glory that fills the Temple on Mount Zion at its dedication (1 Kgs 8.11), that appears in Isaiah's vision of God in the Temple (Isa. 6.1-5), and that is present once again in Ezekiel's vision of the Temple 'filled with the cloud, and the court was full of the brightness of the glory of the LORD' (Ezek. 10.4).

The glory of the Lord might be called a peak experience for biblical writers, in both the literal and the metaphorical sense. In scripture, the glory of God is the almost physical impact in the world of God acting to save his people. And when God enters his creation in salvation and for deliverance, the mountain-top is the biblical place where we should expect to witness his presence. Mighty storm winds and clouds, brilliant light and blazing fire, often comprise the symbology of such a moment.

The imagery of the glory of the Lord is set out dramatically in Psalm 18, whose protagonist cries out to the Lord in anguish, seeking divine help against powerful adversaries. When the help of Israel's God is invoked, it is 'from his temple' that he hears the psalmist's prayer, we are told (Ps. 18.6). The divine response is evoked in powerful imagery of cloud and light:

He made darkness his covering around him,
his canopy thick clouds dark with water.
Out of the brightness before him
there broke through his clouds
hailstones and coals of fire.

(Ps. 18.11-12)

In an imagery that combines darkness and light in a way that seems almost to contradict itself, like the 'bright cloud' of the transfiguration, this psalm tells of the Lord of history stepping into his creation and acting to save. In the tradition associated with the Jerusalem Temple on Mount Zion, it is this same 'bright cloud' of glory that indicates the presence of 'God with us'. Here on the mountain of transfiguration the strong claim of Matthew's Gospel is at one with the equally bold statement that will be made in the Fourth Gospel: 'the Word became flesh and lived among us, and we have seen his glory, the glory as of a father's only son, full of grace and truth' (Jn 1.14).

In the story of Jesus' transfiguration, along with the three disciples we glimpse a vision of the true glory of Jesus, which will appear unveiled in Matthew 28, after Jesus' resurrection. The Gospel narrative in chapter 17 invites us to recognize Jesus as the personal presence of Israel's God, using the imagery of the Temple tradition to make this point. The presence of the symbolic figures of Moses (the law) and Elijah (the prophets) – the two Old Testament figures who were also believed to have experienced mountain-top theophanies – helps to make the same point, the 'law and the prophets' being an expression used to speak of the entirety of God's revelation to Israel. Just as was believed to be the case with Mount Zion, God's revelation is to go forth in its fullness from the place where God is present to effect the inflowing of the nations foreseen by Isaiah. In the transfiguration, we witness the fullness of the law and the prophets surrounding Christ, the presence of God. And in chapter 28, the risen Jesus will commission his disciples to begin the process of gathering in the nations.

There is a final detail in the transfiguration story that adds a further significance to this picture. When in verse

6 the three disciples fall to the ground in fear, Jesus steps towards them 'and touched them', telling them to get up and not to be afraid (see v. 7). In this seemingly insignificant detail of Jesus' touch is one of the key points that Matthew wishes us to notice. In the Old Testament instances of God's presence among his people, such a physical intimacy with the divine would have been unthinkable. Whether it was the unapproachable holy mountain, Sinai, or the more accessible locus of divine presence on Mount Zion, it was impossible to consider the idea that a mortal creature might physically come near, let alone touch the very presence of God. But in the transfiguration story, we witness both the exalted glory and the intimate closeness of God in the person of Jesus.

In the Gospel of John, Jesus will speak of his own body as 'the temple', verbalizing explicitly the pattern of imagery deployed across the Gospel of Matthew: 'Jesus answered them, "Destroy this temple, and in three days I will raise it up." The Jews then said, "This temple has been under construction for forty-six years, and will you raise it up in three days?" But he was speaking of the temple of his body' (Jn 2.19-21). Matthew, like John, understands the person of Jesus to be the very presence in the mundane world of the God of Israel, who made himself accessible to his people – 'God with us' – on the holy mountain in Jerusalem. He is, in himself, the Temple; no longer far off on the high hill, but Immanuel in person.

As the author of the final book of the Bible, Revelation, would discover at the end of his sequence of visions telling of how God is working out the salvation of all the world: 'I saw no temple in the city, for its temple is the Lord God the Almighty and the Lamb' (Rev. 21.22). The message of the transfiguration is the message of the central mystery of the incarnation itself – God is with us, closer than we might ever have dared to hope, in the person of Jesus.

3

The Well: The Third Week of Lent

*Jacob's well was there, and Jesus, tired out by his journey, was
sitting by the well. It was about noon.* (John 4:6)

Whenever I read John's story of Jesus, weary and footsore,
sitting down beside Jacob's well in search of shade and
refreshment (Jn 4.1-42), I am reminded of one of the
most effective lessons in how to read the Bible that I ever
received. I was a newcomer to monastic life, and with others
at that same novice stage was attending a lesson in scripture
study with an experienced senior of our monastery.
He spoke that day about a central fact of life in the Bible
lands: the overpowering force of dry heat. The relentless
sun of the Middle East determines activity for those who
live there to an extent that we softer natives of the temperate
regions of the world can find genuinely hard to grasp. The
difference between life and death can lie in the discovery
of shade, and above all in access to a water source that is
clean and fresh.

The lovely biblical expression 'living water', which
refers in its literal usage simply to water that is flowing, a
moving stream as opposed to a still pool, exactly expresses

what running water and the abundant foliage that generally surrounds it mean for those who inhabit the fierce landscape of the eastern Mediterranean: life rather than death. Cool, shade and growing things, certainly; above all, water in the Bible represents life, and does so with an urgency those of us who live among green fields do not intuitively feel in our bones. Much of the narrative of scripture, both in the Old Testament and the New, has this crucial fact of life as one of its key assumptions.

The psalmist opens Psalm 42, a lyrical prayer of longing for the opportunity to experience God's presence in the Temple on Mount Zion, with the image of the deer thirsting for water:

> As a deer longs for flowing streams,
> so my soul longs for you, O God.
> My soul thirsts for God,
> for the living God.
>
> (Ps. 42.1-2)

The psalm captures perfectly the perspective my novitiate Bible class on dry heat and life-giving water sought to establish: in scripture, we are never far from the question of how and where to find shade and the next drink of water. Because that issue is ubiquitous, water becomes one of the Bible's central and most natural metaphors for the relationship of humanity with God. To be human is to need water, constantly to crave that moistening without which our clay will crumble back into the dust from which it was called into life; and in an exactly parallel way, to be human is to 'thirst for God', without whose spirit, which is the breath of life inspired into the clay taken from the dusty ground, a death yet more terrible will befall the one who was made from the earth.

Like the psalms, the prophetic books delight in the use of the image of water to speak of the life and salvation that come from God. Isaiah equates the one who enjoys God's guidance with a garden supplied by a constant source of life-giving water:

> The LORD will guide you continually,
>   and satisfy your needs in parched places,
>   and make your bones strong;
> and you shall be like a watered garden,
>   like a spring of water,
>   whose waters never fail.
>
> (Isa. 58.11)

As we read Isaiah's words, we are likely moved to exclaim, with the Samaritan woman of John's Gospel as she speaks with Jesus at the well, 'Sir, give me this water, so that I may never be thirsty or have to keep coming here to draw water' (Jn 4.15).

With the third Sunday of Lent, we begin a sequence of Gospel readings from the Fourth Gospel, Saint John, which will continue for rest of the Lenten season. When Jesus sits down at noon beside the well in the Samaritan town of Sychar, the time of day and the location of the event should immediately alert us to the likelihood that John, the great symbolist of the New Testament, wishes us to keep in mind the rich range of signification that attaches to water throughout the scriptures, and specifically to the wells that supply that water. We shall see that water and its vital role in human life is employed both metaphorically and literally by scripture to heighten our consciousness of our need for the divine presence in our lives.

THE WELLS OF SALVATION

The societies in which the texts of scripture were originally written were communities whose lives centred upon a physical resource that has practically vanished from the modern world: the well, and the water drawn from it. In today's First World cultures, wells – if they still exist at all – are quaint folkloric venues for making wishes, tossing coins or snapping selfies. Men and women of Bible times understood the value of wells in quite other ways, as Isaiah's image of the 'wells of salvation' makes plain:

> Surely God is my salvation;
> I will trust, and will not be afraid,
> for the LORD God is my strength and my might;
> he has become my salvation.
> With joy you will draw water from the wells of salvation.
>
> (Isa. 12.2-3)

It is around the well and from the well that a biblical community finds its life; not only in the sense that without the water supplied by the well men and women, flocks and herds and all other living things within the human community will sicken and die; the well is also, because of the need for everyone in the community to have access to it, the centre of social interchange within the town or village that it supplies, a place where influence is exerted, where meetings and conversations occur, bargains are struck, and where future life-partners meet and begin their relationship. The image of the 'wells of salvation' builds on these realities, to suggest a further aspect to the role of wells in the Bible: yes, they are a crucial source of life, and they are a venue of many meetings, but they also function as liminal places where humanity comes into contact with the divine.

The very first well mentioned in the Bible is a good example of this scriptural motif of the water source as the place where we meet the divine. The story in which the first well appears is to be found in the book of Genesis in chapter 16, as part of the Abraham cycle. It concerns the jealousy of Sarai, Abram's wife, directed against Abram's concubine-wife, Hagar, after the latter gives birth to a son. The upshot of Sarai's belief in her own supposedly injured honour is that Sarai so mistreats Hagar that, in desperation, the concubine-wife flees the oasis camp of Abram's clan, taking her infant son, Ishmael, and heading out into territory characterized in the text as 'the wilderness' (Gen. 16.7). This extreme action is tantamount to suicide on Hagar's part, since she has removed herself from all sources of food, water and protection against predators. The Genesis author tells us that Hagar is fortunate enough to stumble upon a spring or well of water in the wilderness; by the time of the writing of Genesis, the site of this well has become known as Beer-lahai-roi, 'the well of the living one who sees me' (Gen. 16.14). This evocative name is understood by the writer to originate in the story he tells of how Hagar, coming upon the well – no doubt we can suppose with considerable relief – is herself discovered by the angel of the Lord.

The 'well of the living one who sees me' in Genesis 16 is the first well mentioned in scripture, just as Jacob's well at Sychar in John 4 is the final such well, and in both cases the well functions as the meeting place between the creator and the human person. The 'angel of the LORD' in the Old Testament ('angel' means 'messenger', and in scripture is more often the designation of a function than it is the name of an order of beings) is frequently a pious biblical circumlocution for God himself; and certainly here in Genesis we are to understand that it is God who comes to meet Hagar at Beer-lahai-roi. This divine intervention saves Hagar's life, and establishes that she is to return to Abram's camp, where she will become the mother of 'offspring that cannot be counted' through her son, Ishmael – the Ishmaelites of later biblical narratives.

Hagar's astonished reaction, 'Have I really seen God and remained alive after seeing him?' (Gen. 16.13) is characteristic of those biblical figures privileged to be encountered in person by the divine presence. It is because of the awe that borders upon terror that God's manifestation inspires, along with the fear that human beings cannot see God and live, that so many biblical encounters between God and humanity begin with the injunction, 'Do not be afraid'. But not only has Hagar 'remained alive' in the sense of having survived the meeting; this encounter has also in fact been transformative. The 'well of the living one' has been, for her, a true 'well of salvation', a source from which there flows in abundance human flourishing, the re-establishment of broken relationships, and a future promise of many descendants – of course, not forgetting the actual water she needed in the desert.

So, in scripture the well is always some kind of meeting place, and often a privileged meeting place with the divine. Biblical wells present an aspect of the connection between our nature as crafted from water and dust, and our creatureliness as springing from the fecundity of divine generation. To be close to water is to be reminded of our need for and our potential openness to the divine; sometimes it is the very occasion of a meeting with God.

While the wells of the Old Testament are places of encounter between humanity and the divine, they are more frequently places where rather more straightforwardly human encounters are depicted. Two particular types of human encounter are regularly depicted in Old Testament narratives involving wells. One set of stories concerns the meeting at a well of different kinship groups or tribes, sometimes in rivalry, and the second type is the initial meeting of future spouses. It happens that the story of Moses' encounter at the Midianite well in Exodus 2 neatly illustrates both kinds of meetings.

At the point in the Moses cycle where this tale occurs, the future liberator of Israel is on the run from Egyptian justice, having murdered an Egyptian overseer who was abusing Hebrew slaves, Moses' kinsfolk. Moses flees from Egypt, and arrives in the neighbouring land of Midian, seeking refuge, and here, we are told, he 'sat down by a well' (Exod. 2.15). In the context of the story, this is a very normal way for a stranger to seek hospitality and to look for work from those coming to draw water. It seems that when Moses arrives at this well, a rivalry is already underway between the seven daughters of the Midianite priest Reuel and 'some shepherds' (v. 17) from another kinship group. Moses sets about resolving the dispute, thereby bringing a third kinship group into the encounter. This is just the kind of encounter between rival clans, each of whom seeks to use a water source, that we find at a number of points in scripture; resolving this type of potential conflict in such a way that all can peaceably draw water is clearly a requirement for prosperity and human flourishing in the communities that cluster around water sources.

In Moses' case, it is in the process of mediating this water-rights dispute in Midian, so that in the end the daughters of Reuel can tend their father's flock, that the fugitive Israelite wins the hand of his future wife, Zipporah, Reuel's daughter (see Exod. 2.15-22). Thus the Moses story does double-duty as an example of both types of typical well scene in the Old Testament: the clan rivalry story, and the narrative of a meeting with a future spouse. We also encounter the motif of the meeting at a well with a future spouse in several of the stories of Israel's patriarchal ancestors. Not only Moses' marriage, but before him the marriages of Isaac (in Gen. 24) and Jacob (in Gen. 29) have been arranged as a consequence of meetings at wells.

We see, then, that the 'wells of salvation' of which Isaiah sings have real physical existence in Israelite society.

It is from the water of the well that human life and the agriculture that supports it are made possible; around the well as the place where water is to be found that there grows up a culture of human encounter and exchange, enabling peaceable relations to exist between families, and bringing different kinship groups into alignment through marriage; while the well as the manifestation of the divine power to bestow life is itself the place where a human being may be graced to encounter God himself. When the psalmist prays a blessing on the home in Psalm 128, it is the waters of the wells of salvation that enable the 'one who fears the LORD' to 'eat the fruit of the labour of your hands'. The household blessed with a secure water source can know that

> Your wife will be like a fruitful vine
> within your house;
> your children will be like olive shoots
> around your table.
>
> (Ps. 128.3)

Fertility of the soil and the fecundity of the family are both closely allied with the provision of the water that represents the blessing bestowed by God upon his people. In John's Gospel chapter 7, Jesus will build upon this perspective to teach, in a promise that paraphrases several Old Testament passages: 'Out of the believer's heart shall flow rivers of living water' (Jn 7.38), and we shall see that this 'living water' plays an important part in the story that forms the Gospel text for this third week of Lent, John 4.1-42.

When in John's Gospel Jesus sits beside the well at Sychar, a Jewish man speaking to a Samaritan woman, we shall see that the Gospel narrative is drawing deeply from the established scriptural motifs in which different kinship groups, men and women, and the human and the divine are involved in encounters beside a water source.

A TREE PLANTED BY STREAMS OF WATER

Our journey to some of the wells of the Old Testament demonstrates that scripture does not understand water as a natural resource in our modern sense, but rather as a manifestation of God's power and generosity. In the Bible, water is an aspect of the creation that only the creator can tame and handle freely. When God answers Job's complains at the end of that most puzzling of Old Testament texts, several of God's poetic sequence of rhetorical questions concern water and God's authority over it: 'Has the rain a father, or who has begotten the drops of dew?' Job is asked (Job 38.28); the implication being, of course, that neither Job nor any other mortal person knows the answer. God's power over water, and over the waters that surround the created cosmos according to ancient worldviews, is a regular feature of the Bible's presentation of the Lord God 'who calls for the waters of the sea, and pours them out on the surface of the earth' (Amos 5.8).

Through God's gift of water, which he alone is able to bestow or to withhold, life is generated and sustained: this simple fact gives rise to a rich symbolism across both Old and New Testaments, in which water and its life-giving qualities come to stand for aspects of the divine activity, and become specifically associated with God's word, spoken by his prophets and written down for us as scripture. Towards the end of the book of Isaiah we read:

> For as the rain and the snow come down from heaven,
> and do not return there until they have watered the earth,
> making it bring forth and sprout,
> giving seed to the sower and bread to the eater,
> so shall my word be that goes out from my mouth;
> it shall not return to me empty,
> but it shall accomplish that which I purpose,
> and succeed in the thing for which I sent it.
>
> (Isa. 55.10-11)

The same chapter opened with the invitation to any who thirst to 'come to the waters', and to drink freely (see Isa. 55.1ff.). Isaiah at this point closely associates the word of God, which in scripture is God's active power at work in the world for the salvation of humanity, with the God-given gift of water that falls from the sky to bring life wherever it goes.

If we turn to the book of Psalms, we can see the water motif being developed in such a way as to associate the *torah*, the law of the Lord, with life-giving water. In a Christian context it is right to read this association as one between the whole of the biblical revelation and the symbol of water. Psalm 1 stands at the opening of the entire book of Psalms; a suitable place for the establishment of key themes that are to be explored in more detail later. This psalmic overture offers a meditation on the relationship between the believer and the *torah* or law of God, the Old Testament term for the self-revelation of God for humanity, in which we are invited to recognize that God's life in us is as fundamental to who and what we are as persons, as vital to our very existence, as is water to the health of the human body or to the continued flourishing of the natural world in which we live.

In Psalm 1, the psalmist places before us a stark contrast between two ways of life, only one of which can – in the last analysis – prove truly life-giving: the way of the just, and the way of the wicked. The just person is characterized as one who delights in the *torah* of the Lord and 'on his law they meditate day and night'. Such persons 'are like trees planted by streams of water'. While the wicked are blown away by the wind as dried-out chaff from a threshing floor, the one who ponders on *torah* is said to be blessed, to be alive and fecund, generative of fertility and prosperity.

Later in the psalter, in Psalm 52, the psalmist will take up a similar theme:

> But I am like a green olive tree
> in the house of God.
> I trust in the steadfast love of God
> for ever and ever.
>
> (Ps. 52.8)

In both psalms, the psalmist likens the relationship between the just one and the Lord to that of a tree and a water source. In both psalms, the way of life that fails to place trust in God as in a stronghold is found wholly wanting (see Ps. 52.7).

The tree of Psalm 52 is growing within the courts of the Lord's Temple, an image that vividly illustrates the trust placed by the just person in the mercy of God that is celebrated in the psalm, and establishes that it is from the presence of God who makes his word accessible to his people from the Temple that all vitality springs. In Psalm 1 the psalmist locates the source of the flourishing tree's life and growth in the relationship between the righteous person and the law of the Lord; because of the 'delight' of the righteous in the law 'the LORD watches over the way of the righteous', while 'the way of the wicked will perish' (Ps. 1.6).

The Hebrew verb translated in Psalm 1.6 as 'watches over' is a part of the verb 'to know'. In Hebrew, 'to know' carries a greater weight than in modern English, and to translate it here as 'watches over' helps to bring out the difference. For God to 'know' or 'watch over' the way of the just, in this psalm and elsewhere, is for God to take regard for, to acknowledge or recognize, to be in a personal relationship with the just one whom God knows. The God of the Bible does not 'know' us simply in the way we might stack up lists of friends on a social media platform, but rather enters into a relationship of mutual trust and active involvement with those who are known. God 'watches over' us, for our salvation.

In Psalm 1 there is a crucial connection between God's knowledge of the just person – 'the LORD knows the way of the just' – and the just one's knowledge of God. In the same way that God does not simply accumulate information when he 'knows', the just one does not neutrally 'know' *torah* as a series of useful facts, but delights in the *torah*, actively pondering it day and night. Just as God 'watches over' the just one, the just one has set about 'watching over' the things of the Lord as they apply to humanity; we are told that 'on his law they meditate day and night' (Ps. 1.2). The word 'meditate', like the term 'know', needs a little unpacking. Unlike the English word 'meditate', which really only suggests a silent cognitive activity, the Hebrew term used here can mean 'murmur', 'mutter', 'groan' or 'growl', or 'cry out'; we might say that it isn't a very intellectual or spiritual word, but rather a description of a repeated physical action. You would not go far wrong if you had in mind the activity of a happy dog with a bone. In Psalm 1, the person who delights in God's *torah* manifests this delight less by a thinking about scripture than by a doing of the word: the enacting of the text, learning it by heart, speaking it aloud, murmuring it repeatedly, growling it 'day and night'.

Thus it is that the image of the tree growing beside the waters of the *torah*, the just person in right relationship with the God of Israel, functions as a key image at several points in the psalter. In Psalm 92, the 'meditation' of Psalm 1 gives way to full voiced shouts of joy, as the psalmist strives 'to give thanks to the LORD, to sing praises to your name, O Most High' (v. 1):

For you, O LORD, have made me glad by your work;
at the works of your hands I sing for joy.

How great are your works, O LORD!
Your thoughts are very deep!

(Ps. 92.4-5)

This is a type of response that we might not immediately associate with the activity called 'meditation', but it is the enacting of an engagement with God's word, a 'watching over' it, that affect the moods and actions of the one who has so engaged. The psalmist is 'made glad', he 'sings for joy' when God's activity is the subject of his thoughts. There are exclamations and cries of delight as the work of engaging with the divine is undertaken.

But there is a contrast within the psalm, which immediately goes on to insist:

The dullard cannot know,
the stupid cannot understand this.

(Ps. 92.6)

We need to keep in mind that in the psalms, and in other parts of the Old Testament associated with what is often called the Wisdom tradition (for example, the book of Proverbs), references to 'the stupid' or 'dullards' have less to do with something negative about intellectual giftedness that might be written on a person's school report than with one's stance *vis-à-vis* God and the scriptural revelation of God's will. In these parts of scripture, a failure to engage creatively with divine truth is characterized primarily as 'foolish'. Psalm 14, for example, opens with the statement: 'Fools say in their hearts, "There is no God."'

The psalmist goes on to say that '[t]hey are corrupt, they do abominable deeds' (Ps. 14.1), but the corrupt abominations follow from the foolishness, they do not cause it. The attitudes and actions of the 'dullard' or 'fool', cut off from the word of life, are like the stunted tree that is not beside the water of torah; it will dry out, wither and be burned or carried away.

By contrast with the 'fool', in Psalm 92 the just one shouts out the loving mercy and truth of the Lord even through the watches of the night. The psalmist sings that the one who 'watches over' the torah may be likened to a flourishing palm tree or a tall cedar:

> They are planted in the house of the LORD;
> they flourish in the courts of our God.
> In old age they still produce fruit;
> they are always green and full of sap.
>
> (Ps. 92.13-14)

It is the life-giving virtue of such a relationship with the word of God that leads to the association in traditional rabbinic exegesis of the torah with water. It's easy to see how such an association might arise, especially in the psalmic context of the image of the tree and its water source. So, for example, in the collection of fourth- or fifth-century rabbinic homiletic reflections on scripture called the Genesis Rabbah, the question is asked concerning another poetic text of the Old Testament, the book of Job: 'What is the meaning of the phrase, "My roots reaching for water"? (Job 29.19). Jacob said, Because I occupied myself with torah, which is compared to water, I merited to be blessed with dew, as it is written, "May God give you of the dew of heaven"' (Genesis Rabbah 66.1).

The image we find in this text is like that of the trees in Psalm 1 or in Psalm 92 whose roots reach for the water of the word of God. The ancient author of this comment associates both the dew from heaven and the waters of the earth with the life-giving *torah* of Israel's God. In such imagery the very text of scripture itself is understood to furnish its readers with access to the wells of salvation.

It comes as no surprise to discover that Christian thought moves in a similar direction. In a letter of the fourth-century bishop of Milan, Ambrose, we discover an extended meditation on the association of the divine revelation with the waters of the earth's rivers and seas:

> The divine scripture is a sea, containing in it deep meanings, and an abyss of prophetic mysteries; and into this sea enter many rivers. There are sweet and transparent streams, cool fountains too there are, *springing up into life eternal*, and *pleasant words as an honey-comb*. Agreeable sentences too there are, refreshing the minds of the hearers, if I may say so, with spiritual drink, and soothing them with the sweetness of their moral precepts. Various then are the streams of the sacred Scriptures. There is in them a first draught for you, a second, and a last. (Ambrose, *Letter to Constantius*)

The picture Ambrose describes of the 'various streams' of sacred scripture is an attractive imaging forth of how we might understand our approach to praying with scripture. The imagery of rivers, streams, fountains and the great sea offers an unusual overview of the whole of scripture – less as a library, the way we more conventionally characterize the Bible, than as a series of intermingled water sources and water courses, sometimes separated one from another, sometimes comingled together, occasionally still pools, often springing heavenward to spray the shores and even the skies. In praying with a scriptural text, one is rarely hearing its words in isolation from the rest of the Bible; our memories will layer pictures and sounds upon one another, and we will be more likely at times to be listening to a chorus of voices rather than a solo performance.

Ambrose's very last sentence bears some pondering – the first, second and further 'draughts' we might draw from the revealed text. It will be clear from all that has gone before that when we 'occupy ourselves with *torah*', to use the rabbinic expression, we are not engaging in a linear, rational process. The psalmist's 'meditation' on the word is less a case of beginning at a certain point, and then logically moving forward, each step following the next with the precision of a chess master moving pieces relentlessly forward on the board, than it is of attending a generous party where the drinks (and possibly also one's head) keep on going around. There is not always great clarity either to the process, or to its outcomes; rather, 'a first draught for you, a second, and a last'. There is a repetitive circling around involved in pondering the word, even perhaps a degree of intoxication.

A very appropriate way to learn how to think about and, more importantly, how to practise scriptural prayer in terms of Ambrose's repeated 'draughts' is to allow oneself to be taught by Psalm 119, the longest psalm in the psalter and the most repetitive. Psalm 119 is written in celebration of the *torah* as the source of true life. It is an extended alphabetical psalm in which there is a section of eight verses for each letter of the Hebrew alphabet, and in each of these sections the Hebrew text of each line begins with the letter the section represents. Such a structural technique does not easily lend itself to a linear development of thought in a piece of writing, although it can be done – but here the psalmist doesn't even make the attempt, as there is only one subject to each of the 176 verses of his poem: how God's human creatures may 'walk in the law of the LORD' (Ps. 119.1). Through the entire length of his poem, the psalmist circles around and back through this one subject, the glory of the *torah*, ingeniously spawning synonyms for his topic – 'seeking God', 'keeping statutes', 'obeying commands', 'learning ordinances', to name but a very few – so as to allow for one draught after another to be taken from the deep well of the word of God.

As a piece of writing, Psalm 119 is perhaps an acquired taste, but as a mode of prayer it is inspired. It is with the very approach this psalm adopts, taking a text and circling around it, murmuring it, pondering it, that we can 'occupy ourselves with *torah*' in the sense commended by the psalmist, and pointed towards by Ambrose's imagery. This taking of a scriptural text and 'watching over' it, circling around it as the psalmist does in Psalm 119, is a fruitful path towards scriptural prayer. The psalmist offers us not only a picture of the tree that has rooted into the fountain of living water, as in Psalm 1 and elsewhere, but also a worked-out example of a way in which the tree can begin to sink its roots towards the water source. When I am a beginner in an area I don't know well, a model to follow can be a considerable boon.

The psalms, we discover, employ an imagery of water as the necessary stuff of life, they establish a pattern of thought about the relationship between the just one and the law of the Lord that equates the *torah* with a source of water for the soul, and they even model ways in which we can involve ourselves in this relationship, learning to allow our dryness to be moistened by the dew of heaven. When Jesus promises 'living water' to the Samaritan woman in John 4, he is not really speaking of water as the physical resource necessary for life, as his hearer seems very quickly to realize. The story of the Samaritan woman at the well is a story about the water of the word of God that enlivens the soul, and how human beings can come into the right relationship with God depicted by the psalmist in the image of the verdant tree in the Lord's Temple.

FOUNTAINS OF LIVING WATER

With the third Sunday of Lent the focus for our Gospel passages shifts to the Fourth Gospel, the Gospel of John. John's Gospel will remain our guide for the fourth and fifth Sundays of Lent. Where Matthew's Gospel is built, often with a sophisticated architecture, out of a series of short narratives of incidents in the life of Jesus and the sayings and stories that form his teaching ministry, John's Gospel employs a very different approach. In John's telling, the meaning and message of Jesus are conveyed through a series of seven great signs (the Fourth Gospel's word for miracles), which Jesus works in order to teach, as well as in lengthy sermon-like discourses, and in several extended dialogues between Jesus and certain individuals or groups he encounters in the course of his ministry. The meeting and conversation with the woman at the well in the Samaritan town of Sychar falls into this last category. Their dialogue is to be found in John 4.1-42.

In the Fourth Gospel no detail is mentioned by chance, but rather John builds up his account of Jesus' saving presence on earth by referencing a wide range of themes drawn from the scriptures familiar to his readers, sometimes referencing them by means of the apparently incidental detail of his narrative. His choice of a well as the setting for his story should lead us to expect that some of the themes we have been exploring in the Old Testament will form threads in the tapestry of this chapter: water as a symbol of life in the broadest sense, certainly, but more particularly the water of the word of God that we have discovered flowing through the texts of the psalms and the prophets.

John begins his story in the Samaritan town of Sychar by identifying the well in that town as 'Jacob's well', and the nearby land as having been given by Jacob to his son, Joseph (4.5-6). In the book of Genesis, Joseph is the saviour of his family in time of famine, having been betrayed by his own brothers and sent away, as if dead, to slavery in Egypt. The author wants us to associate Jesus, who like Joseph will bring salvation to all his brethren as a result of betrayal and degradation, with the figure of his ancestor as we notice this apparently casual reference. The figure of Joseph plays a significant role in the book of Genesis, but scripture does not know of any well specifically associated with Joseph's father, the patriarch Jacob. Rabbinic legend, though, suggests a well associated with Jacob whose waters spring up miraculously and spontaneously overflow, rather doing away with the need for buckets. John surely wants us to have both these points in mind as Jesus speaks with the Samaritan woman about the gift of water, near to land gifted to Joseph, beside a well that legend has it gifts its users with miraculously flowing water. Before either partner in the dialogue of John 4 has uttered a word, there is already a symbolic context established that shapes the meaning of what will soon be said.

Because we have visited the wells of the Old Testament and considered the scenes that typically occur at wells, we are the better prepared for John's account of Jesus' conversation. We can notice that in John 4 the story draws on all three of the 'meeting at the well' themes that we considered earlier. A Jew meets a Samaritan in this story: we recognize that two rival kinship groups are represented here, two groups who in this meeting at a well are in dispute not about water-rights but about the nature of proper worship, and where God is to be found. A man meets a woman beside the well in

Sychar: that the conversation between them turns to issues of marriage should therefore come as no surprise – although if one was not expecting marriage to be a topic of conversation beside a well, Jesus' sudden introduction of the theme of the Samaritan woman's husbands might seem both abrupt and confusing. In the context of this conversation beside a well, John's Gospel also expects its readers to recall the frequent New Testament identification of Jesus as the messianic 'bridegroom', as the Fourth Gospel itself does immediately before this story in the words of John the Baptist: 'He who has the bride is the bridegroom' (Jn 3.29). Here at the well the true bridegroom of Israel offers to a woman whose relationships are irregular – whose people's ways of worship are not those of biblical Israel – a way towards a restored 'marriage', a new relationship with God.

And, of course, much of the dynamic of the conversation arises from the divine identity of Jesus as the word of life, an identity initially unknown to the woman who finds herself, like Hagar of old, arriving at a well in search of the physical water that sustains human life only to encounter the very source of all true life in the person of the living God. John's Gospel intends that we read Jesus' opening words to the woman, 'Give me a drink' (v. 7), in full awareness both of their straightforwardly human content (it is midday, he is tired, and – as the woman points out – he has no bucket with which to draw water) and of the divine irony of the situation: the author of life asks for the gift of life-giving water, the word of God seeks the gift of the word that moistens the heart in the form of *torah*. This irony is just what Jesus points

to in his response to the woman's answer: 'If you knew the gift
of God, and who it is that is saying to you, "Give me a drink",
you would have asked him, and he would have given you
living water' (v. 10). Jesus' answer alludes to the overflowing
well of Jewish legend, possibly also echoing the story of the
well described in the book of Numbers that God caused to
spring up and overflow for the Israelites in the desert (see
Num. 21.16-18). Just as the Lord supplied flowing water
for his people in the wilderness, so Jesus promises the
freely flowing water of life to the Samaritan woman, if she
is prepared to recognize who it is that is speaking to her and
what is on offer.

For the woman, the issue of Jesus' identity is initially
interpreted in the context of the dispute between Jews and
Samaritans to which John several times alludes, and she
takes Jesus' statements as a claim to supplant the common
ancestor of Samaritans and Jews, the patriarch Jacob: 'Are
you greater than our ancestor Jacob?' she asks, with more
than a hint of mockery. Jesus' reply makes it clear that
the one speaking to the woman does indeed 'supplant' the
patriarch Jacob, whose very name means 'the supplanter'
(see Gen. 25.26). Whereas Jacob gifted his progeny with a
miraculously overflowing well, the gift Jesus is offering not
only overflows, it gushes freely within the very persons of
those who are so gifted: 'those who drink of the water that
I will give them will never be thirsty. The water that I will
give will become in them a spring of water gushing up to
eternal life' (Jn 4.14).

Here, the wells of salvation we read of in Isaiah, and
the waters of the *torah* that sustain the lives of the just

like flourishing green trees in the songs of the psalmist, are brought together by Jesus to speak of a renewal of the relationship between humanity and God that goes beyond, that 'supplants', all that has come before in God's dealings with his people. The wells of salvation, the waters of *torah*, Jesus declares, will henceforth be located within the person of the believer – a renewal of the heart, the fulfilment of the promise God makes through the prophecies of the great exilic prophets, Jeremiah and Ezekiel. For Jeremiah, the renewal of God's people will occur through a writing of the word of life upon the heart:

> ... I will put my law within them, and I will write it on their hearts; and I will be their God, and they shall be my people. No longer shall they teach one another, or say to each other, 'Know the LORD', for they shall all know me, from the least of them to the greatest, says the LORD; for I will forgive their iniquity, and remember their sin no more. (Jer. 31.33-34)

The prophet Ezekiel speaks of a 'new heart and a new spirit', the gift of a heart that is filled by God's Spirit so as to know the Lord's ways: 'I will put my spirit within you, and make you follow my statutes and be careful to observe my ordinances' (Ezek. 36.27). It is this very renewal that Jesus promises to the woman he meets at Sychar when he speaks of the 'water gushing up to eternal life'.

The Fourth Gospel will again take up this theme in chapter 7, where the author wishes to make yet more explicit the nature of Jesus' words at the well in Sychar. The events

narrated in chapter 7 occur in the course of the Jewish feast
of Tabernacles, a celebration commemorating the exodus
journey through the desert, when Israel lived in tents
('tabernacles') and was dependent on God directly for both
food and water. The festival featured a daily drawing of water
from the Pool of Siloam in Jerusalem and the ceremonial
use of this water as an offering in the Temple, a moment that
associated the desert journey of Israel with Isaiah's words:
'With joy you will draw water from the wells of salvation'
(Isa. 12.3). John tells us that on the last day of the festival,
Jesus preaches in the Temple:

> Let anyone who is thirsty come to me, and let the one who
> believes in me drink. As the scripture has said, 'Out of the
> believer's heart shall flow rivers of living water.' Now he
> said this about the Spirit, which believers in him were to
> receive; for as yet there was no Spirit, because Jesus was
> not yet glorified. (Jn 7.37-39)

John associates the gift of living water with the gift of the
Holy Spirit, the Spirit of truth who 'will guide you into all
the truth' (Jn 16.13). This is just what Jesus is saying to the
woman of Sychar as he speaks of the true worship, 'in spirit
and truth', the only worship that can bring human beings
close to God (see vv. 22-24). The story John narrates at the
well is a story about the water of the word of God, the word
of truth, that refreshes and renews our innermost selves; a
word that enlivens our spirits with the gift of God's Spirit,
so that we in our turn can become a source of life for others.

There is a direct relationship, we discover, between our openness to God's word, our encounter with the scriptures, and our capacity to enrich the lives of those around us, just as the patriarch Jacob's miraculous well blesses those who approach it with the overflowing waters that bring life to dry dust.

As Israel's historic exile from her native soil came to an end towards the end of the sixth century BCE, the prophet Ezekiel, too, envisaged a restoration of the true worship of God in a renewed Temple, described in great detail in the later chapters of his book. The lengthy visionary passage, in which the prophet is shown the idealized form of a newly reconstructed Temple of the Lord, is found in chapters 40–47. Much attention is paid in the vision to the structures and proportions of the perfected Temple, to which the God of Israel will return to make his dwelling among a restored and renewed people of God. Ezekiel is told: 'Mortal, this is the place of my throne and the place for the soles of my feet, where I will reside among the people of Israel for ever' (Ezek. 43.7). The vision forms a key element in Ezekiel's message of renewed hope for an exiled people; it represents the restoration of a communion of life between Israel and her God in a form that will endure eternally. The final element in Ezekiel's Temple vision involves water flowing from beneath the threshold of the Temple and swelling into a mighty river as it advances:

> As I came back, I saw on the bank of the river a great many trees on one side and on the other. He said to me,

'This water flows towards the eastern region and goes down into the Arabah; and when it enters the sea, the sea of stagnant waters, the water will become fresh. Wherever the river goes, every living creature that swarms will live, and there will be very many fish, once these waters reach there. It will become fresh; and everything will live where the river goes ... On the banks, on both sides of the river, there will grow all kinds of trees for food. Their leaves will not wither nor their fruit fail, but they will bear fresh fruit every month, because the water for them flows from the sanctuary. Their fruit will be for food, and their leaves for healing.' (Ezek. 47.7-9, 12)

In John 4 this imagery of the water of life, the 'spring of water gushing up to eternal life' (v. 14), which like Ezekiel's mighty river gives life and healing wherever it goes, is transposed from the external structure of a Temple building on the holy mountain of Zion to the renewed heart of the believer. Just as we have seen Jesus redefine Israel's hope for the saving presence of God – 'God with us' – from a geographically manifested glory centred upon the Temple mountain to the presence of God within the personal life – the heart – of each believer, so in John 4 Jesus offers to guide each of us 'to springs of the water of life' (Rev. 7.17) that will overflow from our lives to the lives of others, to the enrichment of our world.

In the book of Revelation, John the seer takes up this imagery of flowing waters to speak of how Israel's God is working to renew the created order and bring healing to the nations:

Then the angel showed me the river of the water of life, bright as crystal, flowing from the throne of God and of the Lamb through the middle of the street of the city. On either side of the river is the tree of life with its twelve kinds of fruit, producing its fruit each month; and the leaves of the tree are for the healing of the nations. (Rev. 22.1-2)

4

The Light: The Fourth Week of Lent

*We must work the works of him who sent me while it is day;
night is coming when no one can work. As long as I am in the
world, I am the light of the world.* (John 9.4-5)

Monasteries today probably live no closer to the natural
world's rhythm of light and darkness than any other human
group. Like most people, we make use of artificial light to
banish the night, and close the blinds against the daylight
when we find it too intense for study or meetings. Even
so, we ground our way of living in a sixth-century text,
the Rule of St Benedict, which mediates to us the outlook
and practice of a society far better tuned to the significant
patterns of the day and night than we moderns have
generally become. Arranging life in such a way that sunlight
was available for the tasks that must be carried out with
the care that clear daylight sight allows was simple common
sense in the ancient world, even if this meant reorganizing
the day far more frequently than today's daylight-saving
practices would achieve. Unsurprisingly, in the Rule of St
Benedict, working once the daylight comes and while the
sun allows becomes a metaphor for the life of the Spirit.

In the Prologue to the Rule, St Benedict writes: 'Let us open our eyes to the light that comes from God ... Run while you have the light of life that the darkness of death may not overtake you.' In just the same way, the writers of our scriptures took for granted that since 'Light is sweet, and it is pleasant for the eyes to see the sun' (Eccl. 11.7), the gift of light should stand in many contexts as a sign for the transforming grace of God himself, and especially the grace of finding the right path to tread as we make our way forward through life.

Paul, for example, invokes an imagery of light, a light that he finds both in the creation and in scriptural revelation, as he writes to his Corinthian converts, seeking to expound the unity of God's saving activity in history: 'For it is the God who said, "Let light shine out of darkness", who has shone in our hearts to give the light of the knowledge of the glory of God in the face of Jesus Christ' (2 Cor. 4.6). The very first chapter of the Bible tells us that God's original word of salvation is 'Let there be light' (Gen. 1.3); at the other end of scripture, the final words of salvation in Revelation of the one who calls himself the 'bright morning star' (Rev. 22.16) picture a city which 'has no need of sun or moon to shine on it, for the glory of God is its light, and its lamp is the Lamb' (Rev. 21.23). Light is the most natural and ubiquitous of scriptural symbols for God's saving purpose. The imagery of light features from the beginning through to the very last chapters in the Bible, and as Paul's marvellously achieved theological picture demonstrates, such imagery has the capacity to generate new insights by imaginatively unifying aspects of the history of salvation. God's glorious presence is identified in scripture as the light that enables those who inhabit his good creation to live generously and justly, to walk forward without stumbling, and to see what is really happening before their eyes.

The world of the psalms is one that is regularly illuminated by images of God's light. The psalmist sings of the Lord God as 'my light and my salvation' (Ps. 27.1), the light of God's radiant face shines on his people (see Ps. 80.3), and – like the 'kindly light' of Newman's hymn – God is the lamp that guides the psalmist's feet on the right path (see Ps. 119.105). Psalm 19, 'The heavens are telling the glory of God', considered by C. S. Lewis to be the greatest poem in the psalter, helps us to find our way into the psalmist's understanding of the relationship between God's gift of light in the created order and his self-offering to us in life-illuminating revelation. A hymnic celebration of God in his creation and in his revealed will, the *torah* or law of the Lord, the psalm begins not with a direct cry of praise, but with a picture of a universal liturgy of praise undertaken by the heavenly bodies, united in glorifying God:

> The heavens are telling the glory of God;
> and the firmament proclaims his handiwork.
> Day to day pours forth speech,
> and night to night declares knowledge.

(Ps. 19.1-2)

The psalm builds its picture of the cosmic praises of God as creator around the extended metaphor of a heavenly activity that begins in the first line: the very sky above us and the lights God has set there – the sun, the moon and stars – are eternally involved in a single great act of praise to their creator. As the psalm unfolds, we discover in verses 3-4 that their 'speech', their vocabulary of worship, is in fact silent – 'There is no speech, nor are there words' – and yet, like the light of the heavenly bodies, this silent voice of praise has gone out to the 'ends of the earth'. This psalm inhabits the same universe of the sacred imagination as the author of the book of Job, who – with added sound effects – pictures the creation itself as the moment when 'the morning stars sang together and all the heavenly beings shouted for joy' united in another cosmic liturgy of God's salvation (Job 38.7). Psalm 148 offers a further parallel, opening with a call from the psalmist directed to the heavenly lights, summoning them to enter the liturgy of worship for which their almighty maker set them upon their celestial course:

> Praise him, sun and moon;
> praise him, all you shining stars!
> ...
> Let them praise the name of the LORD,
> for he commanded and they were created.
>
> (Ps. 148.3, 5)

In each of these contexts the biblical writers depict the creation as the arena of the creator's praise. The psalmist pictures the heavens and the earth as a cosmic temple that constantly resounds with praise to the one who established its various elements. The liturgy of the great lights, the sun, moon and stars, which the book of Genesis had depicted in the creation story of chapter 1 as made by God quite independently of light itself, is understood by scripture to exist less for any practical end than it does for the 'glory of God'.

In the next section of Psalm 19 – verses 4-6 – the psalmist continues his poem with a pair of spirited personifications of the sun, the greatest of the lights of heaven, which 'comes out like a bridegroom from his wedding canopy, and like a strong man runs its course with joy' (Ps. 19.5). Wedding imagery is not unusual in a biblical context as a way of speaking of the profoundly spousal connection between the creator and the cosmos, and the imagery of the sun's strength is underlined by the statement that 'nothing is hidden from its heat' (v. 6). In a context where Israel's neighbours frequently not only personified the sun but actually divinized it and practised sun worship, there is probably an element of polemic against such practices in these images. The sun is mighty indeed – we have seen how its dry heat set much of the agenda for life in the Middle East during biblical times – but here even the mighty sun is God's creature, enacting his creative will, and not any kind of independent agent.

Reading on, we find that from verse 7 to the end of Psalm 19, the subject-matter and language of the poem shift in a manner that at first seems abrupt, becoming a series of closely linked verses in praise of the perfection of the torah, God's life-giving revelation to Israel:

The law of the LORD is perfect,
    reviving the soul;

the decrees of the Lord are sure,
making wise the simple.

(Ps. 19.7)

The pattern of the psalmic praise of God's revelation is strongly reminiscent of Psalm 119, the lengthy *torah* poem we explored in the last chapter, and which occurs much later in the psalter. It seems very likely that here in Psalm 19 two originally distinct psalm poems have been brought together at some point in the history of the psalter to create this psalm as we now have it. Nevertheless, the canonical shape of the psalm (the text as we find it in our Bibles today) is perfectly coherent and makes clear sense. In its present form the psalm develops from its opening imagery of a cosmic liturgy of light in praise of the creator, through finding in the light and heat of the sun a symbol of the universal reach of the creator's spousal regard and concern for all of creation, to discovering in the gift of the *torah* of the Lord a way for humanity to live faithfully within the creator's cosmos that 'is clear, enlightening the eyes' (v. 8), a fitting response from the creatures whom God has placed within his ordered cosmos.

The praises of the *torah*, in verses 7-13, when placed in the context of the psalm as a whole, begin to illuminate the significance of the 'speech' and 'knowledge' pouring forth from the heavens at the opening of the psalm. When the heavens tell of the glory of God, we come to realize by the end of the psalm, it is in terms of the law of the Lord that they are speaking. The bridegroom of the skies, the strong man on his course, is responding in his assigned fashion to

the order established by the creator and declared to Israel in
the *torah*. It only remains for the human participants in this
grand design to seek to remain 'blameless, and innocent of
great transgression' (v. 13) by our adherence to the way of
life set out for us in God's word. Just as the great lights
of heaven praise their creator by means of their fulfilment
of what they are made to be, by following their way through
the skies, you and I give glory to God by understanding and
living out the course of life God declares to us through his
revealed word.

The psalm concludes in verse 14 with a prayer in which
the psalmist takes his stand on the rock-like fidelity of the
redeeming God of Israel and prays that he too may be found
acceptable by the creator and law giver:

> Let the words of my mouth and the meditation of my heart
> be acceptable to you,
> O Lord, my rock and my redeemer.
>
> (Ps. 19.14)

In Psalm 19 we encounter two related patterns of the imagery
of God's presence as light. Both patterns can be discovered
throughout the scriptures, and each of them plays a part in
the story of Jesus' sign of the gift of sight restored 'so that
God's works might be revealed' that we shall read about in
the Gospel of the fourth Sunday of Lent: John 9.1-41.

The first pattern of light imagery we notice in the psalm
is one in which the gracious presence of God, his closeness
and his abiding concern for his creation, are delineated by
means of the metaphor of light: 'For the Lord God is a sun

and shield' as the psalmist elsewhere expresses it (Ps. 84.11).
In Psalm 19, the hymnic opening of the poem is informed
by such an imagery of light, manifesting the power and
majesty of the creator. We will explore this pattern of imagery
by examining the psalmic motif of God's radiant face.

In a second pattern of images, the metaphor of light is
found frequently at work as a device to express the efficacy
of God's gift of *torah*, the saving path that guides human life:
'Your word is a lamp for my feet and a light for my path'
(Psalm 119.105). When light imagery is used in the Bible to
glorify God, we are never far from a recognition that God
makes himself present in the creation as lamp and guide
for human life. The imagery of God as light throughout the
psalms is one that places an emphasis on the proactive saving
will of Israel's creator, redeemer and guide. Shining bright
and reaching all parts of the earth, like the light of the sun
itself, for the psalmist the salvation of the God of Israel is
'very near to you' (Deut. 30.14).

LET YOUR FACE SHINE ON US

God's active and abiding concern for humanity and for the
whole of his creation, a concern often illustrated through the
imagery of light as we saw in Psalm 19, is frequently found
expressed in the motif of God's radiant face. 'Let the light
of your face shine on us, O LORD' (Ps. 4.6), the psalmist
prays, invoking the aid of God as deliverer in a situation that
causes him distress. Such an appeal for help in the form of
the light of God's radiant countenance is to be discovered in
several psalms, so it is useful to unpack the meanings of the

motif. The Hebrew expression to 'see the face' of someone
is generally used to mean in a formal sense 'to come into the
presence' of that person, to be near them and be personally
acknowledged by them. So, to 'see the face of God' is an
image of being positively recognized and regarded with
favour by Israel's God.

This is the usage of the expression we find in Psalm 27:
'Your face, LORD, do I seek. Do not hide your face from
me' (Ps. 27.8-9). The psalmist is asking that God should not
'hide his face' or withdraw his favour from the suppliant, but
that he should rather 'lift up his face' in acknowledgement
and kindness. When Jesus speaks in the Gospel of negative
judgement in the form of the statement, 'I never knew you;
go away from me, you evildoers' (Mt. 7.23), or positive
regard in the form of 'Come, you that are blessed by my
Father' (Mt. 25.34), he has this same distinction in mind; the
king lifts up his face towards those who find favour, they see
his face, but from those who are reproached he turns away his
face, or hides it.

The psalmist regularly employs the metaphor of seeking
and ultimately seeing the face of God as a way to speak of the
pious Israelite's hope for divine favour. Frequently, God's face
as a metaphor for his presence and action is closely associated
with his presence in the Temple on Mount Zion. Thus in Psalm
42, the question 'When shall I come and behold the face of
God?' (v. 2) occurs in a context rich in remembered scenes
of worship offered to God in the Temple at a great festival:

how I went with the throng,
and led them in procession to the house of God,

with glad shouts and songs of thanksgiving,
a multitude keeping festival.

(Ps. 42.4)

In this psalm, which perhaps originates in the context of
an Israelite who is in exile from his native land and longs
for the restoration of his nation and her worship, the
taunt of the enemies concerns the capacity of Israel's God
to act and save: 'people say to me continually, "Where is
your God?"' (v. 3). The psalmist offers one of his most
poignant images of longing for divine favour, for the face
of God, in the psalm's opening line: 'Like as the hart
desireth the water-brooks, so longeth my soul after thee,
O God' as the beautiful Coverdale translation expresses
it. 'Like as the hart', like the deer or gazelle, weary from
the chase and yearning for the cooling refreshment of a
watercourse, so my soul is yearning for you, my God. Here,
longing for God is presented as raw need. To be human
in a full sense, this image is telling us, is to experience a
need to see 'the face of God' as basic and urgent as the
hunted beast's need for water in a dry land; we recognize,
with St Augustine, that 'our hearts are restless until they
rest in you'.

We speak colloquially of a person's face 'lighting up' when
someone or something that pleases them comes along. In
scripture, the presence or face of God is itself understood to
be a source of light, akin to the sun at dawn. In the book of
Numbers, we hear of how the sons of Aaron, Moses' brother,
the tribe from whom the Temple priests of biblical Israel
were drawn, are instructed in the proper way to invoke

God's blessing upon their fellow Israelites, in a blessing formula that has become well known:

> The LORD bless you and keep you;
> the LORD make his face to shine upon you, and be gracious to you;
> the LORD lift up his countenance upon you, and give you peace.
>
> (Num. 6.24-26)

The shining face or positive regard of the God of Israel when he 'lifts up his countenance' upon his people is regularly dramatized in language that describes the Lord's face, or indeed his whole person, as a source of light. Thus, in the final blessing before Moses' death bestowed by the patriarch on the Israelites in the book of Deuteronomy, we hear that God manifested himself to them as their saviour with all the brilliance of daybreak:

> The LORD came from Sinai,
> and dawned from Seir upon us;
> he shone forth from Mount Paran.
>
> (Deut. 33.2)

And in the song of Habakkuk, a prophetic poem depicting God's intervention in history to deliver his people, God's 'brightness was like the sun; rays came forth from his hand, where his power lay hidden' (Hab. 3.4). Like Moses, the prophet envisages the glory of the Lord dawning upon Israel to bring the blessing of his presence as surely as day drives back both the real and the intangible fears of the dark night. The psalmist employs a similar image of the breaking light of divine glory in Psalm 50, in which God summons the whole earth to gather before him at his holy mountain: 'Out of Zion, the perfection of beauty, God shines forth' (Ps. 50. 2).

Importantly, these are pictures of the divine initiative exercised to intervene on behalf of Israel, not simply and solely motifs of human aspiration for divine favour. While the image of the face of God is discovered in both contexts, the shining forth of God's face represents God's active power and will to save. The attitude of prayerful longing for the Lord as light is combined with the sure sense that Israel's God is active and involved in the salvation of his people in the imagery of Psalm 130:

> my soul waits for the LORD
> more than those who watch for the morning,
> more than those who watch for the morning.
>
> (Ps. 130.6)

God's shining face, the sign of God acting to save, thus itself comes to be signified by the radiance of the sun at daybreak.

In Psalm 17, the coming of God with the light of dawn is envisaged, perhaps after a night in which the Lord has 'visited' the psalmist to try his heart and test him (v. 3):

> As for me, I shall behold your face in righteousness;
> when I awake I shall be satisfied, beholding your likeness.
>
> (Ps 17.15)

In this psalm we are in the company of a psalmist who is once again beset by difficulty and oppression from 'the wicked who despoil me, my deadly enemies who surround me' (v. 9). The peaceful image of awakening to behold the face of God is less pacific than it might initially appear. For the psalmist to achieve this concluding quiet, there has been an act of divine liberation in response to the plea,

> Rise up, O LORD, confront them, overthrow them!
> By your sword deliver my life from the wicked.
>
> (Ps. 17.13)

Once again, the Christian who prays the psalms must make a transposition between those who perform wicked actions and the attitudes and outlook of wickedness. Nevertheless, it is plain that in the psalms, beholding God's face is not the beatific vision of Christian mystical longing, but is the practical consequence of Israel's God stepping into history so that justice may 'roll down like waters, and righteousness like an ever-flowing stream' (Amos 5.24). It is the God of the exodus whose face is looked for by the psalmist; his countenance has a definite societal dimension, and is to be found in those places where our moral choices make a difference.

This same actively salvific theme is clear in Psalm 80, with its repeated refrain, 'Restore us, O LORD God of hosts; let your face shine, that we may be saved' (vv. 3, 7, 19). This psalm imagines the historic liberation of Israel from Egypt as God's transplanting of a vine into a freshly cleared vineyard, where the new plant has been successfully nurtured by the divine vintner. But, the psalmist asks in complaint,

> Why then have you broken down its walls,
> so that all who pass along the way pluck its fruit?

(Ps. 80.12)

It is the ruined vineyard of Israel that this psalm prays to see restored by the salvific force of God's shining face. Here the imagery of light encompasses both Israel's hope for the future and her capacity to lament derelictions in the present, to cry out to God when confronted by injustice, seeking for a renewed light from heaven in the face of a darkness that threatens to overwhelm. As the psalmist cries out for vindication against Israel's enemies, his hope for Israel is the same as that expressed in Psalm 24:

> They will receive blessing from the LORD,
> and vindication from the God of their salvation.
> Such is the company of those who seek him,
> who seek the face of the God of Jacob.

(Ps. 24.5-6)

The longings expressed in psalms such as these find their future correlate in the fulfilment of God's saving purposes, articulated in both Old and New Testaments. Just as the prophet Ezekiel at the beginning of his ministry was a visionary witness to the departure of God's glory, his saving presence, from the fallen Temple at the point of Judah's downfall (see Ezek. 10), towards the end of his book the prophet witnesses the dawn-like return of Israel's God, shining like the sun in the heavens, to a renewed Zion: 'the glory of the God of Israel was coming from the east; the sound was like the sound of mighty waters; and the earth shone with his glory' (Ezek. 43.2).

As in Ezekiel's vision, an imagery of light encompasses the final vision described in the Revelation of John, the concluding book of the New Testament. In John's vision of the heavenly city, God's now liberated faithful – the pure of heart of Saint Matthew's beatitudes – are said to 'see his face', to be eternally close to God and enjoy the presence for which they have longed: 'And there will be no more night; they need no light of lamp or sun, for the Lord God will be their light, and they will reign for ever and ever' (Rev. 22.4-5).

As the scriptures reach their end, the solar images with which the God who called light into being has been so regularly characterized also come to an end – 'they need no ... sun, for the Lord God will be their light'. The eternal, intimate presence of the saving God himself, now seen 'face to face, as one speaks to a friend' (Exod. 33.11), means that the cosmic liturgy of light that stood duty as the symbol of that divine presence has reached its fulfilment.

YOUR WORD IS A LIGHT FOR MY PATH

As we reflected on the imagery of Psalm 19 earlier in this chapter, we noticed that as well as furnishing us with the motif of seeing the radiant face of God, the metaphor of light is used regularly in scripture as a device to celebrate

God's gift of *torah*, the saving path that guides human life. It is God's light that illumines the path that leads us forward into life.

For Psalm 36, the radiant light that surrounds Israel's God, that flows from God as the fountain of life, is the context for all right seeing and therefore the basis for all just action:

> For with you is the fountain of life;
> in your light we see light.

(Ps. 36.9)

The psalmist understands God's revelation, his word, as the carrier of all truth, goodness and justice; the image of God's word giving light, the *torah* as the light of God showing the way, is a central Old Testament metaphor used to represent that understanding: 'Your word is a lamp for my feet, and a light for my path' (Psalm 119.105).

Psalm 36 continues by contrasting this perspective with the mistaken undertakings of those who are unfaithful to God, who as a result of having 'no fear of God before their eyes' (v. 1) do not see aright. The wicked are pictured as falling and lying prostrate, unable to rise – an image of defeat and rejection, a stumbling to the ground that follows inevitably from a failure to see correctly, through the light of God's word, what actually lies in front of one's steps. 'The way of the wicked is like deep darkness; they do not know what they stumble over', the book of Proverbs tells us, expanding more explicitly on the same point (Prov. 4.19).

The same passage in Proverbs offers a strongly contrasted positive image of the way of life that accords with God's revelation: 'the path of the righteous is like the light of dawn, which shines brighter and brighter until full day' (Prov. 4.18). The psalmist too, especially in the great *torah* psalm 119, employs an imagery of light to characterize the role of God's revealed will in human life: 'The unfolding of your words gives light; it imparts understanding to the simple' (Ps. 119.130).

In an elegantly simple psalm paraphrase, part of a private prayer composed by the seventeenth-century Anglican Bishop of Winchester, Lancelot Andrewes, the author demonstrates a sure sense of how the light of the *torah* is understood by the psalmist:

> Open thou mine eyes and I shall see,
> Incline my heart and I shall desire,
> Order my steps and I shall walk
> In the ways of thy commandments.

Bishop Andrewes combines a series of distinct verses from around the length of Psalm 119 to create this miniature gem of a prayer. The initiative to enable right seeing lies with God, we are told; it is from God that the capacity to see the way is received. It is by God's hand that our hearts are shaped with the desire to follow that way, and our steps guided along 'the way of thy commandments'. The psalmist's belief in the connection between the soundness of the eye and the ordered steps of the righteous shines out from this prayer.

In the New Testament, Jesus employs a number of images of right seeing, making use of the image of the eye itself as a 'lamp', a source of light for the path we follow. This can strike us as a strange way of speaking, until we know that the physics of the ancient world held that sight was only possible because the eye itself in some sense emitted light: 'The eye is the lamp of the body. So, if your eye is healthy, your whole body will be full of light; but if your eye is unhealthy, your whole body will be full of darkness. If then the light in you is darkness, how great is the darkness!' (Mt. 6.22-23).

Jesus is building on the psalmist's perspective, teaching that the one who has learned to see with a sound eye, which is to say an eye informed by the attitudes and practices inculcated by meditation upon the *torah*, will live a life filled with God's generous light. It is because the eye is the source of the light by which we see that it is vital for proper sight that the eye be aligned with the light that comes from God through his word. In Psalm 119 the psalmist prays:

> Turn my heart to your decrees,
> and not to selfish gain.
> Turn my eyes from looking at vanities;
> give me life in your ways.

(Ps. 119.36-37)

Jesus is pointing in the same direction in Matthew's Gospel. Here in chapter 6 he too equates eye and heart, both natural images of what can be most fully alive or most damaged in our lives, to point a stark contrast. On the one hand, Jesus condemns those who set their hearts upon earthly treasure, who fix their eyes upon what the psalmist calls 'vanities'. These are they whose 'whole body will be full of darkness' (Mt. 6.23). On the other hand, he commends those whose 'eyes are awake before each watch of the night ... [to] meditate on your promise' (Ps. 119.148). These are they who seek their treasure 'in heaven' (Mt. 6.20), through being guided in God's 'ways'. This is the attitude of the 'healthy' eye, those whose bodies are 'full of light'. This understanding also helps to make sense of the easily misunderstood injunction to 'tear out' an eye that causes someone to sin (Mt. 5.29), in which Jesus is speaking about a similar set of issues – is the human eye's natural light suffused with the divinely given light of God's word, or has the focus strayed? If so, the body is full of darkness, and action must be taken.

The imagery of the human eye, the lamp of the body, in search of full alignment with the *torah* of God, the lamp for our moral activities, runs through the length of Psalm 119's extended meditation on the law of the Lord as the path to true life. The psalmist seeks to fix his eyes on God's ways (v. 15), his eyes shed 'streams of tears' because the law of God is disregarded by the wicked (v. 136), and his eyes wake in the night to engage with God's will (v. 148). In a similar way, Psalm 37 employs the image of light swelling to the full glare of noonday to speak of the blessing of the one whose eye is aligned with the way of *torah*, who in trust has committed his way to the Lord:

He will make your vindication shine like the light,
and the justice of your cause like the noonday.

(Ps. 37.6)

By implication, the imagery of light dawning and showing the way suggests the possibility of an original state of darkness. In Psalm 112, the descendants of the righteous 'rise in the darkness as a light for the upright' (v. 4). In Psalm 97, 'Light dawns for the righteous, and joy for the upright in heart' (v. 11) at the manifestation in glory of the God of Israel. Both Israel's holy God, and those who seek to accept the way of life that God offers, are associated with an imagery of light.

Israel's prophets look forward to the day when God will take the decisive action he has promised to make plain to all the world that God's way is the path to life, the day we have seen Isaiah paint as a lifting on high of God's holy mountain, so that 'out of Zion shall go forth instruction, and the word of the LORD from Jerusalem' (Isa. 2.3). This moment is also depicted by Isaiah in the imagery of God's light dawning upon a darkened world:

> The people who walked in darkness
> have seen a great light;
> those who lived in a land of deep darkness,
> on them light has shined.
>
> (Isa. 9.2)

The imagery of light, closely associated throughout the psalms with the lamp of the *torah*, and the right seeing of the eye aligned to it, allows the prophet to speak of those who have been alienated from God, and are thus unable to see correctly, coming to accept his gracious intervention and learning what it is to walk in the daylight. Isaiah's imagery is that of a movement from the domain of death into the realm of life, using the imagery of light to speak of this movement. It is this same transition that we shall find at work in the Gospel of John: 'What has come into being in him was life, and the life was the light of all people. The light shines in the darkness, and the darkness did not overcome it' (Jn 1.4-5).

I AM THE LIGHT OF THE WORLD

We saw in the last chapter that the Fourth Gospel, which provides the Gospel texts for the later Sundays of the Lenten cycle, uses a narrative structure distinct from that of Matthew, Mark and Luke. One aspect of this distinctive structure is the sequence of seven 'signs', the miracles that Jesus works in the first 12 chapters of John's Gospel, each of which is followed by a lengthy passage of dialogue (or sometimes simply monologue) in which Jesus teaches how the sign he has worked throws light on the significance of God's saving action in his ministry. The Gospel text for this fourth week of Lent, John 9.1-41, the healing by Jesus of a man blind from birth, is usually understood as the sixth of the seven signs. The Gospel passage we read in the next chapter for the fifth Sunday of Lent (Jn 11.1-45) follows as the seventh sign. It is sometimes suggested that John uses the sequence of seven signs, Jesus' seven miracles, to represent Christ's renewing of the created order of the world, established by God in the seven days of Genesis 1. If we read the Fourth Gospel in this way, the world-changing miracle of Jesus' resurrection, at the end of the Gospel narrative and at the climax of our Lenten journey, is an eighth sign and the greatest of them all: it is indeed an eighth day – signalling a new creation that transcends the original seven-day work of the creator and ushers in a new world.

Jesus' sixth sign, the restoration of sight we read about this week, is the context within which John sets Jesus' teaching, 'As long as I am in the world, I am the light of the world' (Jn 9.5), a saying in which Jesus contrasts the daylight in which work is possible with the coming darkness of night, in which 'no one can work' (v. 4). The binary opposition of light to darkness is one of the pairs of opposed values around which John builds his account of Jesus' identity. This is a Gospel where we frequently encounter pairs of fundamentally contrasted values – life and death, worldly and heavenly, truth and falsehood, slavery and freedom, as well as several others. John's thought-world partakes of the bipolarity we have encountered in the books of Proverbs and Psalms: there is a way followed by the just, who walk in the light of God's *torah*, but the alternative is the way of the wicked, who – as we have seen – will stumble and fall in the darkness that comes with night.

When Jesus teaches about the 'light of the world' here in chapter 9, the reader of John's Gospel has already begun to understand what he is saying with the help of several earlier instances of the same theme. The opening chapter of John's Gospel is redolent of the opening chapter of the book of Genesis in its resounding words, 'In the beginning was the Word, and the Word was with God, and the Word was God' (Jn 1.1). It is here that we first encounter John's association of Jesus with light, and discover the identification that exists for the Fourth Gospel – just as it does for the psalmist – between light and life: 'the life was the light of all people' (v. 4). It is here also that John first establishes the pattern of light shining in the darkness that is part of his central message. For John, Jesus is the 'true light' (v. 9), and illumination by the true light is the way that all people come to walk aright, even as the psalmist taught.

The perspectives of John 1 are developed when Jesus speaks to Nicodemus, a leading Jewish teacher, in chapter 3. In this dialogue Jesus speaks of the judgement that his very presence in the world effects, telling Nicodemus that those who respond negatively to the message and person of the one who himself is light are those who 'loved darkness rather than light because their deeds were evil' (Jn 3.19). Once more we find John building his message upon psalmic foundations; Jesus' teaching draws upon the psalmist's picture of the just who strive for God's light, while the wicked stray ever further into the gloom where no one can walk securely. Jesus, like the psalmist, teaches that an attraction to the light is an attraction to the way of life inculcated by the God of Israel, and that it is for this reason that such a way of conducting oneself is life-giving.

In chapter 8, immediately before the story of the restoration of the blind man's sight, Jesus offers his own explicit identification of himself with the light of God's radiant presence in his *torah* that we have heard celebrated by the psalmist: 'I am the light of the world. Whoever follows me will never walk in darkness but will have the light of life' (Jn 8.12). Here we recognize all of the themes we have followed through the psalms and the prophets explicitly articulated by Jesus as he speaks of himself. The extent of Jesus' bold claim becomes still more apparent when we realize the importance in John's Gospel of statements by Jesus that begin with the words 'I am'. In this Gospel there are several such statements from Jesus, found throughout the Gospel narrative – we shall meet another, 'I am the resurrection and the life' (Jn 11.25), in the next chapter. For anyone listening to Jesus who was versed in the scriptures and traditions of biblical Israel, it would be impossible to hear such statements without having in mind God's self-disclosure to Moses in Exodus 3. Here, on the holy mountain, God imparts God's name to his chosen messenger from the burning bush. Moses has been commanded by God to bear his message to Pharaoh and to the Israelites, and asks for the name of the one who is thus instructing him as a guarantee to those who will hear him: 'God said to Moses, "I AM who I AM." He said further, "Thus you shall say to the Israelites, 'I AM has sent me to you'"' (Exod. 3.14).

Thus when John's Gospel places the 'I am' formula on Jesus' lips, the author fully intends that his readers should appreciate how powerful are Jesus' words. In the course of John's account of the passion of Jesus in chapter 18, Jesus asks the temple police and soldiers sent to arrest him who they are looking for. When they reply, 'Jesus of Nazareth', Jesus says to them, 'I am he'. At this, his opponents fall to the ground (see Jn 18.4-8). This striking detail seems completely inexplicable, unless one knows that Jesus is doing nothing less than uttering the sacred name of Israel's mighty God, and taking that great name as his own. Nowhere

else in the scriptures, other than by God himself, is such a
formula uttered:

> Listen to me, O Jacob,
> and Israel, whom I called:
> I am He; I am the first,
> and I am the last.

(Isa. 48.12)

In chapter 8, we see John bringing the imagery of light
together with the tradition of the sacred name of God.
When Jesus identifies himself in the words 'I am the light
of the world', he is teaching that his identity is one with
that of the God who creates light itself (see Isa. 45.6-7).
It is because the light of *torah* shines in the face of Jesus, the
radiant face of God himself, that those who follow him need
fear no darkness.

In the chapter 9 account of Jesus restoring the sight of the
man born blind, John brings to a dramatic climax the teaching
about Jesus as light that has been growing in momentum
through the earlier chapters of this Gospel. As the chapter
begins, we notice first that Jesus' disciples share the common
assumption of their era that any illness or form of disability
was to be regarded as the consequence of sin (vv. 1-3). This
way of thinking was widespread in the ancient world. It
was a particular issue with regard to sight; the imagery of
walking safely in the light and stumbling in darkness that we
have found in many parts of scripture helps us to understand
that metaphors drawn from physical sight and blindness were
widely used to speak of spiritual insight and its opposite,

spiritual blindness. All too often such metaphors were taken literally, as the disciples' question, 'who sinned, this man or his parents?', makes apparent.

Jesus' unexpected response to the question is similar to his statement in chapter 11 that Lazarus' illness will not end in death but in God's glory (Jn 11.4). The sign that is to be performed for the blind man will reveal God's works in him (v. 3), the works that belong to the light, and which point to the fact that Jesus is himself 'the light of the world' (vv. 4-5). As the story unfolds, we begin to recognize the meaning of what Jesus has said. The man is indeed cured of his physical disability – 'I was blind, now I see' as he says to the Pharisees (v. 25) – but the real sign that a work that glorifies God has been performed is not the physical cure as such.

With a typically insightful irony, the author of the Fourth Gospel has Jesus' opponents make the point for him when they revile the man saying, 'You are his disciple, but we are disciples of Moses' (v. 28). The purpose of the cure of this man afflicted by blindness is that he may come to 'see' the one whom God has sent into the world, Jesus (see vv. 36-38). While the self-proclaimed 'disciples of Moses' remain blinded by their sin, the man who they 'see' as a sinner (v. 34) declares himself a follower of Jesus, and looks upon him with the attitude of worship (v. 38).

This Gospel story draws upon the broad scriptural tradition of an imagery of light applied to God himself and to the way of life that he imparts to humanity to dramatize the prayer of Psalm 119: 'Open my eyes, so that I may behold wondrous things out of your law' (Ps. 119.18).

At the end of the narrative in John 9, Jesus says to the man he has healed and to his other disciples, 'I came into this world for judgement so that those who do not see may see, and those who do see may become blind' (Jn 9.39). The Gospel narrator comments: 'Some of the Pharisees near him heard this and said to him, "Surely we are not blind, are we?" Jesus said to them, "If you were blind, you would not have sin. But now that you say, 'We see', your sin remains"' (Jn 9.40-41).

The whole situation suggested at the opening of the story has been reversed. The man apparently born in sin emerges as the just man; the sighted are declared to be blind; the judgement of God has been enacted. The one who had appeared to be walking in darkness emerges as the one who sees the great light, and seeing the radiant face of God he is empowered to follow the way of God by becoming Jesus' disciple and by worshipping him. Those who were thought to occupy the seat of religious authority are revealed to be stumbling in an impenetrable darkness, since they are in reality those whose eye is not sound, and whose body is, consequently, full of darkness.

John's Gospel takes up the imagery of light, that most natural and immediate biblical symbol for the working of God in our human world, using it to place us within the moment of judgement when God casts down the seemingly mighty from their seats and in their place lifts up the lowly (see Lk. 1.52). God's glory, the manifestation of Israel's saving God within the bounds of his own creation, shines in the face of Jesus because in him the works of God are performed, the judgement of the light is accomplished. In the book of Revelation, this moment in which the light of the glory of God shines in the face of his Son becomes an image of what it will mean for each of us to reach that place ultimately intended for us by the Lord God: 'his servants will worship him; they will see his face, and his name will be on their foreheads. And there will be no more night; they need no light of lamp or sun, for the Lord God will be their light, and they will reign for ever and ever' (Rev. 22.3-5).

5

The Tomb: The Fifth Week of Lent

Then Jesus, again greatly disturbed, came to the tomb. It was a cave, and a stone was lying against it. Jesus said, 'Take away the stone.' (John 11:38-39)

As Lent began, we recognized in the dust of the Ash Wednesday liturgy a sign of the state of our souls as this season of conversion began: often dry of devotion, brittle when we might better bend, lacking some crucial element of the resolution necessary to change. We began to know in our own hearts the truth of the moment when 'the dust returns to the earth as it was, and the breath returns to God who gave it' (Eccl. 12.7). The dust of our humanity must be mixed with the moisture of God's grace and vivified by the breath of his Spirit, the divine wind that renews all creation, if we are to be responsive to the word of life, if our resolution is to be anything more than 'a morning cloud ... that goes away early' (Hos. 6.4). In this fifth week in Lent we stand on the threshold of Passiontide and see Holy Week on the near horizon. Lent, we recognize, does not so much end as slide seamlessly into the commemoration of Christ's suffering and death, and the celebration of his resurrection, the season of repentance overlaid by the liturgies of his passion, crucifixion and the life of the age to come.

The Gospel for the fifth Sunday of Lent (John 11.1-53) presents us with the image of the entombed Lazarus, awaiting the divine wind that brings a vivifying breath to the dust of the earth. Like Lazarus in the tomb, the Christian in Lent waits for a word from the mouth of the creator, at whose command all things are renewed. In the words of Psalm 104:

> When you hide your face, they are dismayed;
> when you take away their breath, they die
> and return to their dust.
> When you send forth your spirit, they are created;
> and you renew the face of the ground.

(Ps. 104.29-30)

Jesus' miraculous raising to life of his friend in John chapter 11 points forward towards his own resurrection, as we have seen is true of the mystery of the transfiguration. The raising of Lazarus also looks backward to all that has gone before in the Gospel story, representing a summation from the author of the Fourth Gospel of the entirety of Jesus' mission to confront the power of sin and death, that desiccating return to the dust which afflicts the core of God's good creation. This miracle of life restored to Jesus' friend stands for the whole of Christ's mission to 'renew the face of the earth'. Perhaps we begin to recognize, in the dryness and unresponsiveness of our own dusty hearts, something of the return to dust that is the power of sin at work. The Christian concept of sin encompasses more than merely the summary of the things we have got wrong. Much more fundamentally, sin is that dusty dryness we recognize in ourselves that regularly turns us away from the offer of the new life Jesus brings, leading us to prefer the aptly named 'devil we know' to the challenge of change. Our sinfulness lies essentially in our *not wanting* more than it does in almost anything that we might positively choose.

In chapter 37 of the book of Ezekiel, the prophet is carried by the Lord's spirit into a vision of a great valley, filled with the dried-out bones of the once great people of Israel. Our desiccated hearts, too, are pictured by the prophet as laid out in the ossuary of that open-air graveyard. Ezekiel's vision concerns the state of God's people in exile, drained of all true life and sick in soul. But his vision also depicts the affliction we discover within ourselves as we struggle to hear the call to conversion.

The vision begins with a disconcerting scene:

> The hand of the LORD came upon me, and he brought me out by the spirit of the LORD and set me down in the middle of a valley; it was full of bones. He led me all round them; there were very many lying in the valley, and they were very dry. He said to me, 'Mortal, can these bones live?' I answered, 'O LORD God, you know.' (Ezek. 37.1-3)

Ezekiel sees in the exiled Israel of his time a community in whom the death-dealing power of sin is all but complete.

This is a people reduced to a valley filled only with bones; in any human sense, all hope has gone from these exiles. In the vision, the bones are not simply dead but utterly dried out – bereft of a future, of connection to God or with one another: 'They say, "Our bones are dried up, and our hope is lost; we are cut off completely"' (Ezek. 37.11). Against this desolate background, the prophet's words cause us to look back to the account of how the creator God first fashioned humanity from the dust of the earth in Genesis chapter 2, as in this later prophetic moment Ezekiel envisions a re-creation from bone dust of the whole house of Israel. It is only by the grace of a fresh act of creation from Israel's God, Ezekiel is telling us, that there can be any future for his people.

Ezekiel is instructed to speak God's word of new creation:

> Thus says the LORD God: I am going to open your graves, and bring you up from your graves, O my people; and I will bring you back to the land of Israel. And you shall know that I am the LORD, when I open your graves, and bring you up from your graves, O my people. (Ezek. 37.12-13)

In Ezekiel's vision the tombs are opened, the valley of bones is transformed by the divine initiative. The scattered bones are brought back together by God's creating word, once more forming the bodies of flesh from which life had fled. The God of Israel instructs the breath of life to return to the people whose hope has perished: 'Come from the four winds, O breath, and breathe upon these slain, that they may live' (v. 9). As the prophet watches, 'the breath came into them, and they lived, and stood on their feet, a vast multitude' (v. 10). Ezekiel speaks an Easter hope to the Lord's people of his own and all subsequent times; a hope we discover even now shining back into the season of Lent as we read his words.

The psalmist's hope that God will send forth his creating spirit to renew the dust of the earth (see Ps. 104.30) is the same hope articulated in Ezekiel 37. It is a hope that will reach its fulfilment in the mysteries of Easter Sunday and the Feast of Pentecost, as the risen one stands among his dispirited and desolated friends, who – hiding behind locked doors and in fear for their lives – have been saying 'our bones are dried up, and our hope is lost', and breathes a life-giving spirit upon them: 'he breathed on them and said to them, Receive the Holy Spirit' (see Jn 20.22). 'Come from the four winds, O breath, and breathe upon these slain, that they may live' is the Lenten prayer we may all make our own as we eagerly long for the festivals of life that are to come.

Such a gratuitous, divinely instituted movement from the dry dust of sin back to the living reality of a verdant creation is among the central image patterns of the Old Testament. It is especially to be discovered in the texts we know as 'lamentations', songs of sorrow whose complaints to God are passionately expressed in poetic form. The book of Lamentations, written to bemoan the political defeat and exile of the people of Jerusalem in the sixth century, is not the only locus of such writing – many psalms also share such an agenda, as does much prophetic writing. A movement from the imagery of the tomb, the grave or the prison pit to that of a new hope founded upon God's salvific activity is the common metaphorical coinage of these texts. In the book of Lamentations chapter 3, for example, we read a complaint expressed in a series of images of defeat, imprisonment and death, 'he has driven and brought me into darkness without any light ... he has made me sit in darkness like the dead of long ago' (Lam. 3.2, 6), which ultimately gives way to a renewal of hope and resolution founded upon the promised salvation that comes from God:

> The steadfast love of the LORD never ceases,
> his mercies never come to an end;
> they are new every morning;
> great is your faithfulness.
>
> (Lam. 3.22-23)

In many of the prayer-poems in the book of Psalms, we can see a similar range of images, and a similar progression of thought. Psalm 143, 'Hear my prayer, O LORD; give ear to my supplications in your faithfulness' (v. 1), offers an example of such a lamentation. Christian tradition dating from the sixth century treats this lament poem as one of the 'seven penitential psalms', of which the best known is the *Miserere*, Psalm 51: 'Have mercy on me, O God, according to your steadfast love' (v. 1). Like Psalm 51 and the remaining penitential psalms, Psalm 143 has been understood by Christians as especially suited to expressing the sentiments of sorrow for sin appropriate to the season of Lent.

Psalm 143 finds the psalmist threatened by enemies who have pursued him and crushed 'my life to the ground, making me sit in darkness like those long dead' (v. 3). As we read this poem, we recognize the same motifs deployed so dramatically by Ezekiel in the vision of the valley of bones – life cast down to the dusty ground, an entry into the darkness of death, the failure of spirit and loss of heart. These motifs abound in the literature of lament. The psalmist implores the renewal of God's favour, thirsting for God 'like a parched land' (v. 6), pleading that God should 'not hide your face from me, or I shall be like those who go down to the Pit' of death (v. 7). Lament poetry is first and foremost a context in which the psalmist recognizes a severe and life-threatening alteration – a very great disruption – in the life circumstances that surround him, and in a series of vividly realized images that cluster around the fear of 'going down to the Pit' or entering 'the darkness of death' cries out to God for help in this situation.

If the conventional shape of an Old Testament lament involves the recognition and expression of the psalmist's fear and horror in the face of the pit of death, his enemies or another form of danger that surrounds him, it also involves a positive resolution of this challenge to the psalmist's life in the form of a divine intervention, which restores the one who prays the lament poem to what Psalm 143 calls 'a level path' (v. 10); the psalmist prays for the restoration of his life to a place where he may once more step forward in safety. In this psalm, the psalmist expects to 'hear of your steadfast love in the morning' (v. 8), to be delivered from enemies (v. 9), and to be guided by God in the 'way I should go' (v. 8). In the pattern of feelings and experiences enacted by a psalmic lament – which takes the one who prays it from the life of the everyday world, through the tomb, the region of the pit of death, finally to arrive at a resolution founded upon trust in the fidelity of Israel's God – we see reflected something of the shape of Jesus' journey through death to new life. These psalms invite us to become involved in that same journey as we pray with them. As Paul will write to the Christian church in Rome: 'we have been buried with him by baptism into death, so that, just as Christ was raised from the dead by the glory of the Father, so we too might walk in newness of life' (Rom. 6.4).

THE REGION AND SHADOW OF DEATH

The public ministry of Jesus in Matthew's Gospel begins in chapter 4, immediately after the arrest of John the Baptist. Matthew tells us that Jesus moves to the town of Capernaum in Galilee, and Matthew, as he so often does, associates this moment with an Old Testament prophecy: that of Isaiah chapter 9:

the people who sat in darkness
have seen a great light,

and for those who sat in the region and shadow of death
light has dawned.

(Mt. 4.16, see Isa. 9.2)

In Matthew's telling of the story of Jesus' life and teaching, it
is into the very 'region and shadow of death' that Jesus steps
as he begins his public ministry, and within that 'shadow'
that he 'began to proclaim, "Repent, for the kingdom of
heaven has come near"' (Mt. 4.17). The season of Lent
involves all of us in recognizing our situation within 'the
region and shadow of death', and allowing the transforming
call to *metanoia*, to repentance, to sound out in our lives.
We are called by Jesus to travel out of the 'far country' into
which, with the prodigal son of the parable, we have strayed
(see Lk. 15.11-32). When, in John's telling of the raising
of Lazarus, Jesus stands before the tomb of his friend, his
summons to the dead man is the same – to come back from
the region and shadow of death: 'he cried with a loud voice,
"Lazarus, come out!" The dead man came out, his hands
and feet bound with strips of cloth, and his face wrapped in
a cloth. Jesus said to them, "Unbind him, and let him go"'
(Jn 11.43-44).

Jesus' command to the crowd, 'Unbind him, and let
him go', seems to suggest something more than simply a
removal of the grave clothes with which Lazarus' body had
been covered for his burial. There is more than a hint here
of Isaiah's prophecy that God's saving work would 'bring
out the prisoners from the dungeon, from the prison those
who sit in darkness' (Isa. 42.7), a prophecy that in Luke's

Gospel is directly quoted by Jesus himself in the synagogue in Nazareth as he begins his mission to Israel (see Lk. 4.16-30). In Luke's account, Jesus tells his hearers that 'Today this scripture has been fulfilled in your hearing' (Lk. 4.21). John is pointing us in the same direction when he places the words 'unbind him' on Jesus' lips. Lazarus has been held captive in the prison-house that Isaiah calls the 'region and shadow of death'; now, to manifest God's glory as the saviour of Israel (see Jn 11.4), Jesus has come to break open the prison.

In the Bible, the 'region and shadow of death' has an almost physical presence. The concept world of the biblical writers was built in other ways than ours, and death is one of the central human realities that was seen differently from the understanding we might expect today. Where we would most probably begin our thinking about the reality of death from within the domain of medical science, the thought-world of biblical times conceptualized death in an almost spatial sense as a place: the land of the dead, or 'Sheol'. This shadow realm, often thought of as in some sense an 'underworld', is regularly pictured for us by the psalmist. Psalm 88, the darkest of the psalms of lamentation, brings us close to those regions the psalmist calls 'dark and deep':

For my soul is full of troubles,
and my life draws near to Sheol.
I am counted among those who go down to the Pit;
I am like those who have no help,

like those forsaken among the dead,
like the slain that lie in the grave,
like those whom you remember no more,
for they are cut off from your hand.
You have put me in the depths of the Pit,
in the regions dark and deep.

(Ps 88.3-6)

Biblical Sheol, or 'the Pit', thought of by Old Testament writers as the underworld region of death, is conceptualized with an imagery largely borrowed from the human experience of placing the bodies of the dead into graves in the earth. Psalm 88 illustrates many of the ideas associated with the 'depths of the Pit': this pit lies somewhere deep beneath the earth, an abode of the dead where the light of the sun cannot be seen. It is a place where human beings are 'cut off from your hand' (v. 5) – where we are no longer held in remembrance by God, and therefore can receive 'no help' (v. 4). This aspect of the land of the dead is a regular concern of the psalmist: 'For in death there is no remembrance of you' (Ps. 6.5). In Sheol, the dead are also removed from the possibility of human fellowship, 'forsaken' as Psalm 88 expresses it (v. 5), or 'passed out of mind like one who is dead' in Psalm 31.12.

The region of Sheol nevertheless somehow impinges regularly upon the lands inhabited by the living, and it is possible – when sick or somehow otherwise adversely afflicted – for the psalmist to say 'my life draws near to Sheol' (Ps. 88.3). This same frightening proximity of the land of the dead to the land of the living is found in

Isaiah 38, where a psalm-like prayer of King Hezekiah of Judah begins:

> I said: In the noontide of my days
> I must depart;
> I am consigned to the gates of Sheol
> for the rest of my years.
> I said, I shall not see the LORD
> in the land of the living;
> I shall look upon mortals no more
> among the inhabitants of the world.
>
> (Isa. 38.10-11)

The king has been severely ill and close to death; his psalm of thanksgiving for his recovery recognizes that he has come close to 'the pit of destruction' (v. 17), dramatically picturing his illness as savaging him like a lion that smashes his bones (v. 13). Imagery of destructive wild beasts is widely employed by the psalmist also, as a way to express the aggressively intrusive power of death to afflict the lives of the living, as here in Psalm 22:

> Many bulls encircle me,
> strong bulls of Bashan surround me;
> they open wide their mouths at me,
> like a ravening and roaring lion.
>
> (Ps. 22.12-13)

The vigour of the bulls and the lions demonstrates that the biblical authors do not see the realm of Sheol as set apart from living human experience. The terrible isolation and darkness of Sheol can erupt into the daylight world, the psalmist regularly discovers, carrying the still living person into 'the power of the dog' and the 'mouth of the lion' (Ps. 22.20, 21). In thanking God for his recovery in Isaiah 38, Hezekiah articulates the close connection between sin and death in biblical thought – the king has recovered from illness because God has forgiven sin, has 'cast all my sins behind your back' (v. 17). His prayer anticipates Paul's statement as he writes to the Christians in Rome that 'the wages of sin is death' (Rom. 6.23).

In the Psalms, and throughout the Old Testament, we discover a pattern of thought whereby threats to the wellbeing of humanity, such as sickness or the dangers posed to life by famine or drought, are described in pictures drawn from the imagery of the realm of Sheol. Psalm 107 offers a series of pictures of the paths to Sheol, by identifying the different regions of life or activities we pursue that can manifest the presence of the realm of death. The psalm is a prayer of thanksgiving to God: 'O give thanks to the LORD, for he is good; for his steadfast love endures for ever' (Ps. 107.1). The psalmist calls upon 'the redeemed of the LORD' (v. 2) to 'thank the LORD for his steadfast love, for his wonderful works to humankind' (vv. 8, 15, 21, 31), a refrain that is repeated throughout the psalm. The redeemed are to thank the God who has redeemed them – brought them back, delivered them – from a range of dire threats to human life. In a sequence of word-pictures, the psalmist describes these threats, understanding them as places or experiences that manifest the realm of Sheol as it impinges directly into the world of men and women.

The first of these regions of death (in vv. 4-9) is the wasteland, beyond the dwellings of humanity. In such 'desert wastes' – as we have noted in earlier chapters – the threat to life is real. Those who wander 'in desert wastes, finding no way to an inhabited town' (v. 4), are very likely to die of hunger or of thirst, as we saw would have been true for Hagar in the book of Genesis had she too not been redeemed by the Lord. In the exodus from Egypt, Israel as a people was guided safely by the Lord through this deadly landscape: 'the great and terrible wilderness, an arid wasteland with poisonous snakes and scorpions' (Deut. 8.15). It is a place where only the direct intervention of God can provide for the continuation of life.

The second group of the redeemed (vv. 10-16) have been held captive, 'prisoners in misery and in irons' (v. 10). The lot of the captive, assigned to a life 'bowed down with hard labour' (v. 12), or held in the prison pit of 'darkness and gloom' (v. 14), is rightly judged to be life-threatening by the psalmist. This was the lot of Joseph in the Genesis narrative, treacherously betrayed by his own brothers and sold into a life of slavery from which the Lord ultimately redeemed him (see Gen. chapter 37ff., and Ps. 105.16-22). A common way to hold someone captive in the ancient world was to use the simple expedient of a deep pit in the ground – the similarity of such a prison to a grave was far from accidental.

The third threat to life that Psalm 107 explores (vv. 17-22) is sickness, akin to the illness King Hezekiah experienced, which causes a sufferer to draw 'near to the gates of death' (v. 18). Many attitudes towards physical illness and also to disability that we encounter in the scriptures have to do with the view that these aspects of human life are among the manifestations in the living human world of the influence of the realm of the dead. Those who have been thus afflicted and are now restored are called to praise the one who 'delivered them from destruction' (v. 20).

The fourth and final manifestation of Sheol explored in this psalm (vv. 23-32) is the domain of the 'mighty waters' (v. 23), the oceans with their storms that lift up the waves so that they mount to heaven and fall into the deep (see vv. 25-26), causing mere humans to stagger like drunkards. In the biblical mind, as we saw in chapter 3, only God has power over water in any circumstances. This is most especially true of the waters of the oceans, where God performs 'his wondrous works in the deep' (v. 24). The seas and oceans have a primordial quality in scripture, and are frequently portrayed as essentially inimical to human life, as in Psalm 69 where God is invoked to save the psalmist 'for the waters have come up to my neck' (Ps. 69.1). 'I have come into deep waters, and the flood sweeps over me' (v. 2), this psalm continues. In the same way, Psalm 107 understands the oceans, braved by those who venture 'down to the sea in ships' (v. 23), as a realm of danger which at any moment can threaten those who go there with a voyage to Sheol. More than once, the psalmist sings of the unlimited power of

Israel's God in terms of his authority over the mighty waters, as here in Psalm 29:

> The voice of the LORD is over the waters;
> the God of glory thunders,
> the LORD, over mighty waters ...
> The LORD sits enthroned over the flood.

(Ps. 29.3, 10)

The four domains of death explored by Psalm 107 help us to understand more fully what Matthew's Gospel is asserting when it presents Jesus as the one who comes bringing light into the 'region and shadow of death' (see Mt. 4.12-17). For scripture, it is always true that 'in the midst of life we are in death', as the burial service from the Book of Common Prayer puts it. Because sin is at work in human life, and the consequence of sin is deadly to human wellbeing, Jesus' mission to overcome sin can be rightly understood as a stepping by the Lord of life into a realm of death, a place associated with the Sheol of the psalmist, 'the darkest valley' (Ps. 23.4).

Psalm 107's four dark regions of death are each assailed and overcome by Jesus in the course of the Gospel stories: the wilderness forms the location for the narrative of Jesus' temptations in each of the first three Gospels, and we have seen how in the desert Jesus was victorious where Israel failed in bringing the obedient fidelity of a son of God into this realm of death; in proclaiming 'release to the captives' (Lk. 4.18) and binding the jailer of humanity, the 'strong man, fully armed' (Lk. 11.21), Jesus has opened wide the gates of the prison of Sheol; in accounts offered by all four Gospels we see Jesus driving back the realm of death in the conquering of sickness and disability as he heals many who have fallen because of ill-health into the grip of Sheol; and when Jesus calms the stormy raging of the Sea of Galilee (Mt. 8.23-27), and walks on the waters (Mt. 14.22-33), we hear that 'those in the boat worshipped him, saying, "Truly you are the Son of God"' (Mt. 14.33), since he is demonstrating the authority that only God himself can employ to command the mighty waters of the great deep, the fourth and final gate of Sheol identified by the psalmist.

Each of the Gospel narratives in the New Testament has as its central claim the triumph of God in Jesus over the power of sin and death in human life, the destruction of the 'region and shadow of death'. We saw in chapter 2 that the New Testament identifies the person of Jesus with the 'holy mountain of God', Mount Zion, where the God of Israel made himself present among his chosen people. The prophet Isaiah, who spoke of the exaltation of the holy mountain to become the locus of a pilgrimage of all nations seeking the law of God, also speaks of how Mount Zion, the place where 'God is with us', will be the location of the great feast that celebrates God's victory over the power of Sheol, when God will 'swallow up death for ever':

On this mountain the LORD of hosts will make for all
     peoples
a feast of rich food, a feast of well-matured wines,

of rich food filled with marrow, of well-matured wines
    strained clear.
And he will destroy on this mountain
the shroud that is cast over all peoples,
the sheet that is spread over all nations;
he will swallow up death for ever.

(Isa. 25.6-8)

In his first letter to the Corinthians, Paul has this passage
from Isaiah in mind as he writes of the resurrection of
Christ: 'Death has been swallowed up in victory' (1 Cor.
15.54). He goes on to quote from Hosea 13.14, another
prophetic author who looked forward to the redeeming
power of Israel's God over the realm of death: 'Where,
O death, is your victory? Where, O death, is your sting?'
(1 Cor. 15.55). The imagery of the tomb, the realm of Sheol,
underlies many of the great claims of the Easter kerygma
in the New Testament, in which we find the power of the
grave definitively overcome in Jesus: 'thanks be to God,
who gives us the victory through our Lord Jesus Christ'
(1 Cor. 15.57).

I AM THE RESURRECTION AND THE LIFE

As we saw in the previous chapter, John's Gospel deploys a
rhetoric of light and darkness to speak of the conflict with
the power of the tomb, of Sheol, that Jesus is undertaking:
'The light shines in the darkness, and the darkness did not
overcome it' (Jn 1.5). Against the darkness of the realm of
the tomb, Jesus identifies himself in John's Gospel as 'the

light of the world' (Jn 8.12), and at the beginning of the
Lazarus story in chapter 11 again employs the imagery
of light to associate the 'sign' he is about to perform, the
seventh and greatest of his signs in this Gospel, with his
mission to overcome sin and conquer death: 'Are there not
twelve hours of daylight? Those who walk during the day do
not stumble, because they see the light of this world. But
those who walk at night stumble, because the light is not in
them' (Jn 11.9-10).

As in chapters 8 and 9, John uses the imagery of light
in this saying to connect the works Jesus is carrying
out with the shining of the radiant face of Israel's God,
made visible to all through the gift of *torah*, his revealed
will, which bestows the ability to see and walk aright. Jesus
is presented in John's Gospel as the revelation of God in
his own person – 'the light of the world' – whereas those
who reject him and what he is doing are attempting to
'walk at night', and will stumble and fall to the ground.
The stark choice of which Jesus speaks here is between
the light of day and the darkness of night, between the
life that he himself brings from God and the deadly realm
of Sheol.

The delay Jesus introduces at the beginning of the
story of the death and raising of Lazarus – he waits two
days before responding to the message about his friend
from Mary and Martha (vv. 3-6) – can easily be misread
if one seeks a contemporary 'psychological' reading of the
Gospel narrative, asking for example what interior state
of mind or emotion caused Jesus to delay his response.

John demonstrates no interest in Jesus' states of mind; his concern is rather to underline Jesus' comment that 'This illness does not lead to death; rather it is for God's glory, so that the Son of God may be glorified through it' (v. 4). As we have seen, for people of biblical times, the power of death reaching into the world of living people was an active and fearful force. We saw how Psalm 107 vividly depicts four of the paths that lead to the gates of death, one of them being illness. In verse 4, Jesus asserts categorically that in Lazarus' case the path being trod leads not to Sheol, the pit, but to God's glory, a glory in which he participates. Jesus delays attending the sickbed of Lazarus precisely in order to show that in this illness the sting of death is already overcome, because his friends will see the light of the world and are not walking in darkness.

As Jesus goes on to tell his disciples: 'Lazarus is dead. For your sake I am glad I was not there, so that you may believe' (v. 14). Jesus' gladness, once again, has nothing to do with Lazarus' suffering or the sisters' anguish. He rejoices rather that Sheol is now unlocked, and Lazarus' death is being transformed into a sign of the resurrection life to come. One of the teaching techniques John's Gospel regularly employs, one that can confuse the reader at first, is to have Jesus act and speak from the perspective of the Word who is God, while the disciples, or other interlocutors, behave and talk on a much more mundane level, often failing to appreciate what is being said to them.

When Jesus arrives in the village of Bethany, Lazarus is entombed and has been dead for four days (v. 17). The

Gospel's chronology helps to make the point that the seventh sign, while it points to the resurrection of Jesus himself, is not identical with it. Jesus calls Lazarus from the tomb after four days, thereby demonstrating that the path of illness had a direction other than death on this occasion. But in spite of Jesus' miracle, his friend will die again one day. By contrast, Jesus' resurrection on the third day means that he 'will never die again; death no longer has dominion over him' (Rom. 6.9).

It is from this perspective that Jesus teaches Martha and the readers of John's Gospel, 'I am the resurrection and the life. Those who believe in me, even though they die, will live, and everyone who lives and believes in me will never die' (Jn 11.25-26). Jesus completes his statement by asking Martha, 'Do you believe this?' (v. 26). As in Jesus' other 'I am' sayings, such as the 'I am the light of the world' that we examined in the previous chapter, Jesus here invokes the holy name of God, claiming it as his own. Such statements are intended by John to be understood as Jesus' most solemn teaching about his own identity and about the nature of God himself. By completing the teaching with the question he puts to Martha, Jesus connects the claim he makes for himself with the need for faith to be at work in the believer. It is those who, like Martha, can answer, 'Yes, Lord, I believe' (v. 27) to what Jesus says here who will participate in the victory over Sheol that Jesus here proclaims.

When Jesus says 'I am the resurrection', he is not only speaking about the miracle that he is about to perform, nor is he only pointing forward to the events that are about to occur at Passover in Jerusalem later in John's Gospel – the events of his passion, death and resurrection – although the gathering opposition to Jesus is detailed later in chapter 11 and the raising of Lazarus will provoke the High Priest Caiaphas to utter his unconsciously prophetic declaration that 'it is better for you to have one man die for the people than to have the whole nation destroyed' (v. 50). Jesus is also specifically referencing what Martha has just called 'the resurrection on the last day' (v. 24), and saying that he embodies this wonderful promise of God in his own person.

The doctrine of the resurrection of the dead 'on the last day' only appears explicitly in the texts of the Old Testament very late in the religious history of Israel, beginning from the second century BCE. It is grounded in the biblical hope that after the future completion of the destiny of God's created cosmos, God will initiate a change in the created order so fundamental that it can only be scoped in a very broad way, and then only in the language of pictures and symbols. Building on much earlier scriptural insights such as the expectation of a 'new exodus', the renewed time of freedom from slavery for God's people that we encountered in chapter 1, Israel's seers began to look towards an intervention of God in history so profound that it could only be called a new act of creation. The Bible begins to long for a new creation in which the sinful consequences of humanity's original disobedience to God have been banished, and a new relationship with the

creator has been inaugurated. We see this hope beginning
to emerge in contexts like the visions of a renewed Temple
in the books of Ezekiel or Isaiah (see Ezek. 40ff. and Isa.
2.1-4), or in Isaiah's repeated prophecy of the 'new thing'
that God is about to perform:

> Do not remember the former things,
> or consider the things of old.
> I am about to do a new thing;
> now it springs forth, do you not perceive it?
>
> (Isa. 43.18-19)

In the New Testament this same hope is explored in the
book of Revelation's visionary understanding that God
is working to remake his world, to make a 'new heaven
and a new earth', beginning from the 'holy mountain' of
Jerusalem, the place where God dwells among his people
in a spousal relationship more wonderful than even the
intimacy of the original Eden: 'Then I saw a new heaven
and a new earth; for the first heaven and the first earth
had passed away, and the sea was no more. And I saw the
holy city, the new Jerusalem, coming down out of heaven
from God, prepared as a bride adorned for her husband'
(Rev. 21.1-2).

The biblical literature in which this set of beliefs about
the new creation is worked out is often given the name
'apocalyptic', a word that in a biblical context refers to
an unveiling of new things, a revealing of what was not
known before and has to be disclosed by God rather than

discovered by human insight. It is within the emerging set
of apocalyptic beliefs and hopes about God's 'new thing'
that we discover the expectation of a 'resurrection on the
last day'. The clearest statement of Israel's faith that her
creator God would also be the final redeemer of humanity
in the face of the power of death is to be found in the
book of Daniel: 'Many of those who sleep in the dust of
the earth shall awake, some to everlasting life, and some
to shame and everlasting contempt. Those who are wise
shall shine like the brightness of the sky, and those who
lead many to righteousness, like the stars for ever and ever'
(Dan. 12.2-3).

It is this picture of the resurrection, which takes up and
develops the imagery of Ezekiel's vision of the valley of
bones, that Martha is talking about when she responds to
Jesus' assurance that Lazarus 'will rise again' (v. 23), and
it is with this doctrine and all that goes with it that Jesus
explicitly identifies himself in his statement to Martha, 'I am
the resurrection and the life' (v. 25). But unlike Martha,
who – in common with the apocalyptic writers of the Old
Testament – thought of the renewal of creation and the
'resurrection on the last day' as a distant hope, Jesus is
teaching that in his own person and in his activities, God has
already begun the new thing that the prophets foretold, and
that in him the new heaven and the new earth have begun to
appear, here and now. Jesus' conflict with Sheol, reported
by the Gospel writers through his miraculous challenges
to the power of sin and death at work among humanity, is
understood in John's Gospel to be the beginning of the new

heaven and new earth; Jesus tells Martha that what she has thought of as the distant 'last day' is in fact happening in her today, and right under her nose.

It is significant that Jesus is speaking of himself and not of Lazarus when he speaks of 'the resurrection'. The seventh sign of John's Gospel, the raising of Lazarus, like the raising of Jairus' daughter in Matthew, Mark and Luke (see Mt. 9, Mk 5 and Lk. 8), stands as a signal pointing to the work of destroying the power of the tomb, the power of Sheol, that Jesus is undertaking in his mission to Israel, and as such it identifies Jesus as the beginning of the new creation. But these miracles of the raising of the dead are never designated in scripture with the term 'resurrection'. The apocalyptic hope for the resurrection of the dead does not envisage a return to a form of earthly existence, such as that of Lazarus, in which it would make any sense for someone to plot 'to put Lazarus to death' (Jn 12.10). Those who rise to 'everlasting life' (Dan. 12.2) in the resurrection of the dead will be able to say, with the risen Jesus, 'I was dead, and see, I am alive for ever and ever' (Rev. 1.18). The resurrection 'on the last day' is not conceptualized in the Old Testament as an event that can or will take place within the established created order of the cosmos.

The term 'apocalyptic' has acquired a popular general usage as meaning 'momentous' or 'catastrophic', largely because the apocalyptic biblical texts that speak of the resurrection of the dead regularly portray this hoped-for moment of new life as preceded by a fundamental and all-embracing change in the created order; this change features catastrophic

or momentous events such as those mentioned in Mark's
Gospel, chapter 13:

> the sun will be darkened,
> and the moon will not give its light,
> and the stars will be falling from heaven,
> and the powers in the heavens will be shaken.
>
> (Mk 13.24-25)

So 'resurrection' as a biblical category in Jesus' time refers
to God's gift of a new and everlasting life in a completely
renewed creation, not to a miraculous restoration of life
and health to someone who has lived in and is returned
to the present created order. When Jesus speaks of the
'resurrection', it is this yet more glorious concept that he is
talking about.

   The sign of the raising of Lazarus is narrated by John in such
a way that it both points forward to Jesus' own resurrection
at the end of the Gospel, and yet is very definitely distinct
from it. All the signs, the miracles that Jesus works in John's
Gospel partake of this double aspect: each of them speaks
of the conflict Jesus is engaged in with the power of sin and
death present in the good creation: sight is made new, food
and drink are provided in abundance, nature is restored to its
proper order, sickness is cured and even death is banished.
Yet at the same time, each sign points beyond the reality of
the present age into an unimaginable new age to come. In the
seventh sign, the raising of Lazarus, this orientation towards
the future is especially strong, as Jesus' self-identification as
the resurrection and the life makes plain.

MY GOD, MY GOD, WHY HAVE YOU FORSAKEN ME?

It may be that the single line from the book of Psalms that is most familiar to all Christians is the opening verse of the great psalm of lamentation, Psalm 22: 'My God, my God, why have you forsaken me?' In the psalter, these words open the most eloquent and harrowing of the psalmist's accounts of the human encounter with the realm of Sheol, a descent towards the pit of death that is recounted in a language dominated by an imagery of the power and bitterness of the tomb. These same words are, of course, reported by the Gospels of Matthew and Mark as having been spoken by Christ on Calvary: 'When it was noon, darkness came over the whole land until three in the afternoon. At three o'clock Jesus cried out with a loud voice, "Eloi, Eloi, lema sabachthani?" which means, "My God, my God, why have you forsaken me?"' (Mk 15.33-34).

The words from the cross are capable of being understood in several ways, and the most natural of these is as a cry of abandonment emerging from a very dark place of suffering and anguish. It is impossible not to experience Jesus' cry as expressing the horror of the suffering that leads to his death. But all the Gospel narratives have to be read at more than one level simultaneously. In John 11 the same Jesus who has just taught Martha that 'I am the resurrection and the life' is 'greatly disturbed in spirit and deeply moved' (v. 33); he weeps at the tomb of the man he is about to call back to life (v. 35). John speaks of a Jesus who is the new creation of God in his own person, and who weeps in the face of human suffering – both facets are elements of the one story. In the Gospel accounts of the passion of Jesus, we are reading about almost inconceivable human suffering, and at the same time about one who 'knowing all that was to happen to him, came forward' (Jn 18.4) to undergo that suffering. The same point can be made about Jesus' cry from the cross. The Gospel writers expect their readers to recognize the source of these words in the book of Psalms, and to understand that Jesus, most especially here as he suffers the pains of death, remains the one who holds seven stars in his right hand and from whose mouth comes the sharp, two-edged sword that is God's word (see Rev. 1.16). Jesus is not reduced to one who suffers a personal agony and calls out merely on his own account: his cry is the cry of the Word of God, and he cries out by speaking the fulfilment of God's word.

The Gospel narratives of the crucifixion of Jesus make the same point as they deliberately draw us back again and again to Psalm 22: in this forcefully realized account of a descent towards the world of the Old Testament Sheol, the psalmist several times reaches for an imagery of human degradation that the evangelists will employ to illuminate the meaning of the events on Calvary:

> But I am a worm, and not human;
> scorned by others, and despised by the people.
> All who see me mock at me;
> they make mouths at me, they shake their heads;
> 'Commit your cause to the LORD; let him deliver –
> let him rescue the one in whom he delights!'
>
> (Ps. 22.6-8)

Not only the mockery and taunting of the crowd that surrounds Jesus on the cross is discovered by the Gospel writers as anticipated in the sufferings enumerated by the psalmist, but some of the physical anguish of crucifixion is found in Psalm 22:

> my mouth is dried up like a potsherd,
> and my tongue sticks to my jaws;
> you lay me in the dust of death.
>
> (Ps. 22.15)

Psalm 22 also offers a connection to the crucifixion when the sufferer's clothing is claimed by his executioners, who gamble for the choice items they take from him:

> I can count all my bones.
> They stare and gloat over me;
> they divide my clothes among themselves,
> and for my clothing they cast lots.
>
> (Ps. 22.17-18)

When the Gospel narratives of Mark and Matthew place the opening words of Psalm 22 on the lips of the crucified Jesus and, along with John, relate the sufferings of the passion story to those described in the course of the psalmist's lament, the reader is placed in a position similar to that of Jesus' first disciples, who are told so frequently by Jesus 'that everything written about me in the law of Moses, the prophets and the psalms must be fulfilled' (Lk. 24.44). The text of this psalm is understood by these New Testament authors as a divinely inspired scriptural insight into the significance of the cross of Christ – each of these Gospel writers intends us to read this psalm as we approach Passion Sunday and Good Friday, and to recognize that the journey of the psalmist towards the gates of Sheol offers a window into the course of Christ as the paschal mystery begins to unfold.

The account of Calvary in John 19, traditionally read in church as a major part of the Celebration of the Passion of the Lord on Good Friday, does not place the opening line of Psalm 22 on the lips of Jesus, as Matthew and Mark do. But, in common with them, it is apparent from the detail of John's narrative that he knows this psalm has a message that his readers need to discover. What John's Gospel does offer is a parallel to Psalm 22 that is not found in the other Gospels. When Mark and Matthew have Jesus begin Psalm 22 with its terrible cry of pain, they may well suggest – although they do not actually say – that Jesus also prays the rest of the psalm, arriving at the psalmist's triumphant conclusion, a shout in celebration of the God who is exalted high above all earthly powers. John – who we know has identified Jesus as himself the presence in a world of sin and darkness of the light that brings resurrection life, the beginning of the new creation – does not repeat the cry of desolation that opens Psalm 22. But John does seem to point his reader towards the end of the psalm, with its cry of fulfilment, as Jesus dies on the cross: 'When Jesus had received the wine, he said, "It is

finished." Then he bowed his head and gave up his spirit'
(Jn 19.30).

The words 'It is finished' are not intended by John as an
expression of defeat muttered by a victim of cruel injustice;
this word from the cross speaks rather of the final fulfilment
of all that had to take place in Jesus' mission in the region
and shadow of death, and brings to the mind of one who
is reading Psalm 22 the psalmist's concluding words, 'he
has done it'. From verse 22 to the conclusion of the psalm
in verse 31, the greatest of the Old Testament laments is
transformed from a harrowing account of tragedy into a song
of triumph, a rejoicing in the God of Israel who has delivered
the psalmist from the depths of Sheol and who will now rule
over all nations, over the living and those who were dead,
for ever. In John's Gospel, Jesus, who is 'the resurrection
and the life', dies fulfilling these scriptural words of triumph;
the task of breaking the power of the tomb and inaugurating
the reign of the God of life over a renewed cosmos has been
accomplished. 'It is finished', all is fulfilled, and the Lord God
'has done it':

> All the ends of the earth shall remember
> and turn to the LORD;
> and all the families of the nations
> shall worship before him.
> For dominion belongs to the LORD,
> and he rules over the nations.
> To him, indeed, shall all who sleep in the earth bow down;
> before him shall bow all who go down to the dust,

and I shall live for him.
Posterity will serve him;
future generations will be told about the LORD,
and proclaim his deliverance to a people yet unborn,
saying that he has done it.

(Ps. 22.27-31)

ACKNOWLEDGEMENTS

Scripture quotations are from the New Revised Standard Version Bible: Anglicized Catholic Edition, copyright © 1989, 1993, 1995 the Division of Christian Education of the National Council of the Churches of Christ in the United States of America. Used by permission. All rights reserved.